Suzette Llewellyn and Suzanne Packer
with Friends

Still Breathing

100 Black Voices on Racism,
100 Ways to Change the Narrative

HarperInspire, an imprint of HarperCollins Christian Publishing

1 London Bridge Street
London SE1 9GF

www.harpercollins.co.uk
www.harperinspire.co.uk

First published by HarperCollins 2021.

A catalogue record for this book is available from the British Library

ISBN: 9780310126737 (Hardback)
ISBN: 9780310126744 (ebook)
ISBN: 9780310126751 (Audio)

Design and Typesetting: Kieron Lewis (kieronlewis.com)

Printed and bound by GPS Group in Bosnia and Herzegovina.

MIX
Paper from
responsible sources
FSC™ C007454

FSC
www.fsc.org

This book is produced from independently certified FSC™ paper
to ensure responsible forest management.

For more information visit: www.harpercollins.co.uk/green

Suzette Llewellyn and Suzanne Packer
with Friends

Still Breathing

100 Black Voices on Racism,
100 Ways to Change the Narrative

INSP:RE

CONTENTS

To my parents, Angela Maria Jackson and
Berris Oswald Jackson, as I pass the torch of
resilience and courage to my son Paris.

Suzanne Packer

To my parents, Lauria and Ulrica Llewellyn, who came
to England with hopes and dreams, and for my daughters,
Viva and Bonnie, who embody them.

Suzette Llewellyn

BEFORE YOU READ

Some of our writers, in expressing their experiences, have been forced to use words that were deliberately chosen to belittle, humiliate, and dehumanize them. If we did not include these words in their stories, we would be dishonouring the writer's voice and their truth.

We do not intend any offence to the reader, and certainly do not promote or advocate the use of such words. Our intention in creating this book is to widen understanding and hope.

Foreword
by Sir Geoff Palmer OBE

The video showing the harrowing 8 minutes and 46 seconds, which ended with the death of George Floyd in 2020, brought to the attention of the world the injustice that black people have suffered for hundreds of years. Historically, this kind of racism was given false 'academic justification' by philosophers such as David Hume and Immanuel Kant. For example, Hume said, in 1753, 'I am apt to suspect the Negros to be naturally inferior to whites.' Later, Kant linked this falsehood to the fiction he promoted as 'the Theory of Race'.

These untruths have enslaved and denied the rights of black people for centuries. Race is a social construct, a cultural lie. Cultural lies are passed on and are difficult to change. However, racists should note that racism is based on falsehoods and is a crime against humanity.

This excellent collection endeavours to address and overcome racism by relating in a unique way the experiences of distinguished black people, who have suffered racism in their lives and work. Their achievements and those of other black people prove that Hume's prejudice is a lie. The statements of those who have contributed to this innovative book must be read to understand how racism damages lives and our society. All of the contributors are part of the good fight that will consign racism to the past. Our ancestors fought in chains; we can surely fight without them.

We cannot change the past but we can, within and beyond our schools, change the consequences of the past for the better, by means of education. This book is part of that education.

Introduction

There is no doubt that 2020 will be a 'year for the ages'. In hindsight, it seemed to be born bad, with the Australian bushfires still burning from June 2019 and, in December, a novel coronavirus being identified in China. Yes, 2020 did not start well, and as time marched on it grew into a behemoth of a year.

A global pandemic was declared and millions of citizens were confined to their homes to prevent the spread of the virus. As travel ceased and people sat at home, a spotlight fell on another age-old virus that had long infected the world.

February 2020. Ahmaud Arbery was out jogging in Glynn County, Georgia. when he was hunted down and shot. Despite video evidence identifying them, his murderers had yet to be charged. Ahmaud was a black man; his killers were white.

May 2020. Christian Cooper was bird-watching in Central Park, New York City,

'To bring about change, you must not be afraid to take the first step. We will fail when we fail to try.'

ATTRIBUTED TO ROSA PARKS

when a white woman objected to him asking her to obey the bylaws of that area and put her dog on its lead. That woman used the shield her whiteness afforded her to call the police and claim that her life was being threatened by an African-American man. That woman knew her white life was valued above that of Christian Cooper.

Some hours later in Minneapolis, before scores of witnesses, a policeman knelt on the neck of George Floyd and suffocated him. George Floyd used the last of his life's breath to call out to his dead mother.

Yet again there was video evidence, but no one was immediately charged.

These incidents joined decades of encounters in which black lives were brutalized on the altar of white supremacy. This time, as had happened before, there was an outcry, fire in the streets, looting and marching; there were protest and calls for justice.

I AM THE DAUGHTER OF SURVIVORS AND I HAVE THRIVED.

I HAVE THRIVED AND I WILL NOT LET THE PAIN OF RACISM SOAK UP JOY

SUZETTE LLEWELLYN

But now these calls were joined by other cries from around the world and, with all this taking place during a global pandemic, everything was heightened. As we saw folk protesting in masks it seemed the virus of racism might finally be taken as seriously as the coronavirus.

'I'm empowered, exhausted, devastated and exhilarated in equal measure.' This is how a friend described her feelings about the protests that followed as a direct response to the murder of George Floyd.

We started to talk about how we had been impacted personally by racism in this country.

We felt the need to respond. We *wanted* to respond. This book is our response.

We decided to tell our story and invited ninety-eight people of African descent to share their experiences of racism with the world. These would be compiled and presented in book form. These testimonials would demonstrate the harm and damage experienced by the contributors and, at the same time, show the way each survivor of racism and prejudice had managed to transform that trauma into strength and potency. >

The result is *Still Breathing*: a legacy book where 100 voices of African descent come together to share their stories and struggles, with a focus on changing the narrative and the world for future generations.

Why I can't join you

As we invited more people to join us on this book project, we found that the reasons to accept the invitation were as interesting as the reasons not to. The following replies tell their own story.

'I don't think I'll be able to contribute to your project right now because I am also wearied about reliving some of the experiences so frequently.'

'I am very moved by these pieces. It's almost too much to have to dredge up memories, which I'm sure is the case for many. I don't think I can find the proper time and headspace for your needs. My suspicion is I don't want to go there.'

'I wish you guys luck with this. It will be a very powerful book, but also very painful. So much talent neglected, and thriving despite that, is for me simultaneously moving and enraging, and saddening and encouraging.'

'Thank you for this. I do wish the book well, but I don't want to speak of my many, many experiences of racism, sexism, ageism. That would be two books.'

100 VOICES OF AFRICAN DESCENT

A FOCUS ON
CHANGING
THE NARRATIVE
AND THE WORLD FOR FUTURE
GENERATIONS

'I am a person that does not look back and give power to those negative experiences. I hope you understand. I want systemic reforms in every sector. This is the only way forward I believe. The fight continues.'

'I'm not going to contribute. Mostly because I think I've been very good at burying negative experiences.'

'I found June BLM really emotionally exhausting, and I've got lots of other stuff going on right now that I don't actually have the brain space to dig all of that up too.'

'My experiences could be interpreted by many as paranoia because I never had in-your-face blatant racism/racist encounters, as far as I can remember. Maybe because I was generally very quiet at school, and just got on with my work, and got the results for the school, this made them very happy with me. So, I think my encounters are essentially "soft" (but significant to me), because no one has ever said to me, "You can't do that because you are black.'

We get it, and thank them for their honesty.

With a little seed
of imagination, you can
grow a field of hope.

AFRICAN PROVERB

Part I
Imagination

Kwame Kwei-Armah	Judith Jacob
Damian Paul Daniel	Josette Bushell-Mingo
Pamela Nompumelelo Nomvete	Michael Obiora
Jason Pennycooke	Benedicta Makeri
Sharon D. Clarke	Stevie Basaula
Halina Edwards	Beverley Knight
Sheda, of Holda Poetry	Suzette Llewellyn
Trish Cooke	Sistren
Jocelyn Jee Esien	Merissa Hylton
Sharon Walters	Neequaye 'Dreph' Dsane
Josephine Melville	Jacob V. Joyce
Rakie Ayola	Lettie Precious
Errol Donald	Chinonyerem Odimba
Veronica McKenzie	Treva Etienne
Suzanne Packer	Elliot Leachman
Mzz Kimberley	Bumi Thomas

Kwame
Kwei-Armah OBE

ACTOR, PLAYWRIGHT, SINGER, DIRECTOR
AND BROADCASTER

To quote Toni Morrison, 'the very serious function of racism is distraction. It keeps you from doing your work. It keeps you explaining, over and over again, your reason for being.' I use this quote because writing about racist experiences I've had in my life, and how I overcame them, is so much harder than I originally thought. Not because of the absence of them, but because in order to free enough mental bandwidth to not have racism define my life or temper my dreams, after each and every battle with that pernicious beast, I tend to dismiss the racist experience from my active memory and place it under lock and key, somewhere deep within the nether regions of my mind. Therefore, finding that particular key and unlocking that door has proven as challenging as remembering the password to an app I created back in the day.

THE
EXPERIENCE

I CHOSE TO EXPLORE HERE IS ONE WHERE THE FIRST LINE OF BATTLE IS WITH YOURSELF

But I shall endeavour to because avoidance, no matter how valid the reason, runs the risk of devaluing your tools, of deskilling, or even worse, creating a narrative absence of how to, when to, or why to, for the generations to come.

My childhood was underscored with the physical manifestations of white supremacy, so I will avoid recalling one of those because the basic mechanism of fight or flight were the only options available, and I imagine we are all very familiar with those.

The experience I chose to explore here is one where the first line of battle is with yourself. The negotiation we often have is when the attack is draped under the cover of plausible deniability. Where you are forced to ask yourself, is it me personally that caused that reaction, or is/was it rooted in the 'R' word? Such is the power of systemic racism that the very weapon of enquiry can often turn back on itself, and make the victim blame themselves for the attack they just endured. That disables your power to respond, and in doing so, allows the aggressor to live another day without the moral reckoning their actions deserve.   >

I BELIEVE THE
REAL FIGHT
IS AGAINST

So here we go. I was once invited into a newly formed group of gatekeepers and powerbrokers dedicated to positive advocacy. At my first meeting I realized quickly that I was the only non-white person in the group. That happens to me often (less so nowadays, I'm pleased to report), so I noted, but paid it little mind. It became clear after a few meetings, however, that my views or suggested action points were being given very little space and at times – and I've heard female colleagues speak of this in all-male spaces – the exact idea, often with as close to the same words that I had used, when articulated by someone white in the group, was given ample space to catalyse and mature. I let that go on for maybe two months, because before I call any action 'racist', I need to have discounted every other possibility. Call it giving people enough rope to either elevate or to hang themselves with.

When all else had been eliminated, I stopped attending the meetings, without informing the chair. I knew that my absence would be noted, not because I was valued, but because the group's now conspicuous whiteness rendered them exposed to criticisms of racism.

As suspected, they enquired as to why I had stopped attending without notice. I explained that I had created a new advocacy group, whose aim was to invite people whose opinion it truly valued; but most importantly, we had created a manifesto and action plan that we were about to present to a philanthropic group that would further *all* of our aims and objectives. The reason we could move so quickly was because this new group was truly diverse in gender, sexuality, and racial terms, had no real hierarchy to speak of, and therefore was filled with people whose whole life experiences were outside of the box, thus radically inclusive actions came naturally to us.

'The very serious function of racism is distraction.'

TONI MORRISON

SYSTEMIC RACISM

What was amazing to me was that within a few weeks, I had heard of several 'people of colour' being invited into the first group, and within a month or so, the chair was a black woman. The sector now had two powerful groups advocating for it, both diverse, both catching the parts that the other may have missed, ultimately benefiting the sector as a whole. When the battle being advocated for was won, both wrapped up shop. I use this example because I believe the real fight is against *systemic* racism. Win that battle, and the walls of Jericho come tumbling down.

Kwame Kwei-Armah OBE.
Actor, playwright, singer, director and broadcaster.

On TV, Kwame is best known as the popular paramedic, Finlay Newton, in *Casualty*. His award-winning play *Elmina's Kitchen* was staged at the Garrick Theatre in 2005, making it only the second play in history to be written by a person of African descent to be staged in the West End. Kwame is currently the Artistic Director of the Young Vic Theatre, in London.

Damian
Paul Daniel

DIRECTOR OF PHOTOGRAPHY

Apart from being called 'Black Sambo' in the playground, the first time I can remember experiencing racist abuse was when I was eight years old. I'd been to the sweet shop and was walking home when a group of four teenage skinheads started shouting, 'black nigger', and began to chase me. I was very scared and ran as fast as I could. Luckily, I was close to home and got through the door before they could reach me.

We lived in a mainly white area of southwest London. One day, when I was eleven or twelve years old, I was walking along the Upper Richmond Road with my friend Matthew, who is white. A car drove slowly along the opposite side of the road. There were two men in the front and a woman in the back seat. As they passed us, they shouted out of the car window. I heard them say, 'Fucking black', 'You nigger', 'What the fuck are you doing here?' By this time I was more used to racists, but Matthew was shocked and upset. He asked me if it made me wish I was white. I said no.

I was in the Scouts and one time we went to a camp in Rochester, Kent.

ne evening we went to a local takeaway ourselves. When I was waiting outside, man in a parked car wound down his ndow and threw chicken bones at me. was shocked and surprised but didn't anything to anyone about it.

These are just a few instances and they ade me realize I was different from my white ends, but I don't remember ever wishing I as white, as my parents had instilled a sense pride in me and made me aware of my lture from an early age. I used to think that ese occurrences didn't really bother me, but e fact I can remember them in such detail, these years later, shows they did make an pact. My experiences of racist abuse have at nes made me attempt to second-guess white people, especially working in film and TV wonder if they are making assumptions abo me simply because of my skin colour.

I have always had the confidence believe I can achieve anything I set out do, knowing that the only barrier to movi ahead is me. But if I'm brutally honest do think that prejudice has held me ba in my career. I'm not saying that it's alwa conscious bias or racism, but time a time again, if the choice comes down hiring me, a black man, or a white pers of the same pedigree, the white pers gets the job. I'll apply to be the Director Photography, but only be offered the r of Camera Operator, if at all.

THEY MADE ME REALIZE I WAS

DIFFERENT

ROM MY

WHITE FRIENDS

Things have changed since I was growing in the 1970s, but racism is still going ong. It may not be as overt and possibly t even conscious, but its shadow is still ere looming, and for every report, for ery attack you hear about, you wonder out how many more you don't.

Damian Paul Daniel.
Director of photography.

Damian's work spans documenta drama, commercials, and features. He s the award-winning documentary *Aga the Tides* and the Royal Television Soci nominated *Black Hollywood: They've Go Have Us*, and he is regarded by BAFTA a 'Brit to Watch'.

Pamela
Nompumelelo Nomvete

ACTOR, AUTHOR,
STORYTELLER

My Letter to a Racist

My name is . . .

I'm sorry, is this thing on?

Testing: one two, one two.

Oh right, yes of course. You can't hear me.

Why is that?

How is it you only seem to see me, I'm only visible to you . . . I mean, I suddenly have purpose when you need me to explain your racism.

Your misuse of power and total disregard for my dignity seems to thrive on hearing all about the pain and degradation your misbehaving has caused me.

When it comes time for that fix, suddenly I am given a platform and, like an obedient marionette, I take centre-stage and dance . . . for . . . you . . . still.

See, when I wake up in the morning, I never have to remind myself that I am black and female and yet . . . I only seem visible when you make me acknowledge this obvious fact.

I didn't write the manifestos that would ensure my displacement as you so diligently constructed my annihilation, my humiliation.

Slavery.   Colonization.   Genocide. Apartheid.

However you phrase it.

Why am I always the one expected to unpack it, enlighten you by showing you my scars, so all over again, I am forced to dance to your discordance.

My name is . . .

I'm sorry, is this thing on?

Testing: one two, one two.

My name is . . .

Oh, that's right, you don't care to know because you already have a name for me. which is why you can't – or won't –

Hear

My

Name

Refuse to pronounce it as I have taught you, but keep insisting it is inappropriate and oh so ugly and complicated.

Funny though: when it comes time for you to self-flagellate, suddenly you make your feeble effort to say my name so I can climb onto your stage and do my dance, so you can feel enlightened. There you go with your frown of concern and fallacious opinion of me and my pain. I didn't create my pain.

You need to tell me why you have scorched my body and soul with your hate. Born of what? Ignorance?

Disgust?

Power?

Shame?

Greed?

Anger?

Foolishness?

My name is . . .

Is this thing on?

Testing: one two, one two.

My name is . . .

Libero to you.

My actual name is

Uhuru.

Now let me enlighten you.

Free.

Can you say that?

No?

No.

Because that name is mine.

It was not manufactured by your sticky hands or your poisonous countenance. Let go.

I am no longer available for your party.

I am

Malkia.

I am the painter.

The choreographer.

The creator.

Turn this thing off.

Pamela Nompumelelo Nomvete.

Actor, author, storyteller.

Pamela was born in Ethiopia to South-African parents. She has performed on stage with the Royal Shakespeare Company, the Royal National Theatre, and the Royal Court. A star of the hit television show *Generations*, Pam is a recipient of the FESPACO Best Actress Award.

Jason
Pennycooke

ACTOR AND CHOREOGRAPHER

RACISM IS NOT
A BLACK ISSUE
IT'S A
WHITE
ISSUE

'Racism is not a black issue, it's a white issue that has an adverse effect on black people.'

I read this quote somewhere and it resonated with me, so I decided to post it. At least 100 of my followers (largely majority white) *unfollowed* me. It made me think, why would that statement offend? Ah! I know: 'Reverse Racism' – whatever that is.

Definition: The concept that affirmative action and similar colour-conscious programmes for redressing racial inequality are a form of anti-white racism.

The concept is often associated with conservative social movements and the belief that social and economic gains by black people in the United States, and around the world, cause disadvantages for white people.

However, there is little to no empirical evidence that the white race suffers systemic discrimination. Racial and ethnic minorities generally lack the power to damage the interests of whites, who remain the dominant group in the USA and the UK. Claims of reverse racism tend to ignore such disparities in the exercise of power and authority, which scholars argue constitute an essential component of racism. **>**

STILL THE STRUGGLE FOR
EQUALITY AND

So, how can it be anti-racism? It can't!

Dear White People,

What you're actually experiencing from me and my socially oppressed brothers and sisters is the adverse effect of the racism your race has inflicted on us over hundreds of years, either personally or intergenerationally. It literally haemorrhages from our very souls. The trauma passed down through our ancestral genes.

Christina Sharpe writes in her book, *In the Wake,* 'We exist in the resistance of the wake', and goes on to explain that, 'black lives are swept up and animated by the afterlives of slavery and materiality of the wake, the ship, the hold, and the weather'. The sign of the slave ship marks and haunts contemporary black life in the diaspora, and the spectre of the hold produces conditions of containment, regulation, and punishment that are genetically passed down from

generation to generation and manifests itself as unexplained trauma, mental health, etc. Anti-blackness and white supremacy only perpetuate said trauma and in turn, oppression.'

So you see, we 'exist in its resistance'. It is part of us and always will be. There are estimated to be thousands, if not hundreds of thousands, of lost black souls at the bottom of the Atlantic – 'the wake' – because they knew death would be better than bondage. And there is a collective consciousness that binds us.

So, if you want to take offence to my opening statement, know that your offence comes from a place of subconscious guilt and complicity, and not discrimination. Your following doesn't define me, but you're unfollowing definitely defines you.

By way of giving one of many modern-day examples, as opposed to just the former 'ancestral' one. When I replied, 'I've never

BASIC HUMAN RIGHTS RAGES ON

been arrested,' after being asked by the police officer who had pulled me over recently, his reply was, 'What? Never?' If I have to explain what's wrong with that statement, go back a few paragraphs and start again.

Now, we are in the vortex that is 2020.

Still the struggle for equality and basic human rights rages on. Black lives matter even more, especially with the sprinkle of a highly contagious virus that is singling out black and ethnic minorities. How convenient.

So maybe you'll find it easy to understand how wary most black folks get when Bill and Melinda Gates say that black people and minorities should be first to be immunized when a vaccine is ready. It makes us question their true intention.

Wake trauma is not the Gates's intention; it's the reason for suspicion about their intentions.

Though we have been here since the first-known *Homo sapiens*, 'Lucy', breathed life on this earth, and we'll be here until it ceases to exist . . . when all that's left is 'the wake'.

A few of my favourite quotes:

'Do not allow yourself to be defeated. They can put the chains on your body, never let them put the chains on your mind' (Kunte Kinte, *in* Roots, *Alex Haley*).

'If there's no enemy within, the enemy outside can do us no harm' (African proverb).

'You can't wear a crown, with your head held down' (Beyoncé, *from her album*, Black is King).

Jason Pennycooke.
Actor and choreographer.

Jason is a multiple Olivier Awards nominee. He is best known for his extensive work in musical theatre, including his portrayal of Thomas Jefferson in *Hamilton*.

Sharon
D. Clarke

ACTOR AND SINGER

Never Give Up my Pride

Listening to parents, my aunts and uncles.

'Lawd, England cold, and de tree dem dead.

Everyting grey!'

They stayed and forged a way, hoping for us, a better day.

Despite all the grey.

Turned away from doors,

Mum being asked, 'What's it like to live in a house, after living in a cave?'

Running from Teddy Boys

Police beat up my uncle on his own doorstep, for loitering with intent, as he, drunkenly, tried to find his key.

Story after story, each one ingrained in me.

Each one a piece of armour, for my stories to be.

Age 6: 'Fat little black bastard!' My parents sat me down and had 'the Talk!'

12: A man spits in the street, looks at me: 'Nigger, pick that up!'

13: Russell shoves me, calls me a black bastard. I know I'm suspended as he hits the deck.

A director asks me, 'How does one pick cotton?'

A writer asks me to be more black, because 'He *knows* black people!'

After a gig, the club owner says, 'I've never slept with a black woman. Sleep with me and my friend . . . I'll pay you.'

Sleeping in the theatre, cos the digs I'd booked were gone when I showed up, suitcase in hand.

On the next tour I saved myself a lot of shoe leather with, 'Hi, I'm a black woman and I'd like to ren–'

Just can't get a taxi, my hand held high. Black b– cabs just pass me by.

Buildings and monuments, in the city that I love, remind me it was built on my forebears' blood.

Hatred staring me down, from NF, BNP, EDL eyes.

'Go back to where you came from, bitch!'

'Born in Tottenham,' say I, with Jamaican pride.

October '85, Cynthia Jarret died.

So many names, not a 'Stateside' problem. Right here, we continue to say their names.

Cherry Groce

Roger Sylvester

Smiley Culture

Joy Gardner

Jimmy Mubenga

Julian Cole

Sean Rigg

Stephen Lawrence

Anthony Walker

STORY AFTER STORY, EACH ONE

INGRAINED

IN ME.

EACH ONE

A PIECE OF ARMOUR,

FOR MY STORIES

TO BE

Across the water,

8 minutes, 46 seconds. The world watches as yet another black man dies.

Say his name: George Floyd. We all hear his cries.

And now there seems to be a shift, and the world marches with us.

Black lives matter! Black lives matter! >

So how do you feel? How can we help? Can you help us to help you? We just want to help. We've got to change, we're going to make changes, be anti-racist, be diverse, we're going to implement change.

So how do you feel?

I feel empowered, and devastated, and hopeful, and so, so angry.

George Floyd's murder has opened your eyes, but can you have really been so blind?

WE'VE BEEN DYING FOR A LONG TIME,

This shocking news is as old as colonialism.

We've been dying for a long time, crying for a long time, rising up and fighting for a long time, raising our voices, biting our tongues, holding it in for so damn long, holding on, keeping on, trying to be strong, needing to be strong, having to be strong.

*'I feel empowered, and devastated,
and hopeful, and so, so angry.'*

SHARON

CRYING FOR A LONG TIME, RISING UP

AND FIGHTING FOR A LONG TIME, RAISING OUR VOICES, BITING OUR TONGUES

And I know, by God, I am strong.

For I stand on the shoulders of wisdom and strength. And their deep roots anchor me.

They endured, rose through it, made their mark, and equipped me to navigate it, head held high, forge my way and never give up my pride.

Sharon D. Clarke MBE.
Actor and singer.

Sharon has received three Olivier Awards for her contributions to British theatre and is best known for her roles in *Doctor Who* and *Holby City*.

Halina Edwards

FREELANCE DESIGNER AND RESEARCHER

On Beauty

When I was 18, I was out with a friend in a club that I used to love going to before moving to London. We went outside for some fresh air when I overheard someone tell a joke. I turned around to join in the conversation. The guy took one look at me and said, 'I don't date black girls. Sorry, I just don't find black women attractive.' This rant spewed on for around ten minutes, which then continued to evolve about the blackness of my skin and his preference for black women

he found attractive who were closer to the complexion of white. Surrounded by all his white friends and my white friend at the time, it felt like a lifetime. In our drunken state of mind, we all stood there in shock and it felt like the world stood still.

I didn't realize the weight that comment had on me, and how much it has stuck with me wherever I go. Panicked that a guy I find attractive won't find me attractive, because he may not see me under the dim nightclub light. Scared to make a move just in case the verbiage of what I was told when I was 18 will be repeated in my twenties. Instead, I keep quiet and try to manage the anxiety I feel in my chest and my racing mind, keep it at a minimum, so my night isn't ruined, trying to prepare myself for a comeback if anyone says that to me again.

It made me wonder though: in another world, another country, another location, I would be the most beautiful woman in the world to someone.

It led me into an investigation of black women who were so beautiful they even had to cover their hair when they were enslaved, as the slave owner found them too

Hairpieces: Halina Edwards | **Photograph:** Avesta Keshtmand

attractive owing to the way in which they fashioned their hair. In parts of Nigeria and other West African countries, hairstyles can depict if a woman is single, married, or looking for someone. Canerows were used to help enslaved people escape from slavery. Often, they were used as a map to help enslaved people escape to freedom. Our hair is strength.

It made me look into the relationship with my hair. When I was 19, a friend at the time cut my transitioning hair (relaxed hair that is chemically straightened to the new growth of my Afro hair), and I cried. I cried my eyes out at the fact my natural hair was short, and I – at the time – equated long hair with beauty. My hair used to be in long braids to my back, as I was growing my hair out to a length that would pass my collar bones. My friend at the time didn't understand why I was so upset, and I couldn't find the words to articulate how I was feeling because the overarching feeling was that I felt ugly.

It's taken a few years, and it's an ongoing, never-ending process of learning to love my hair at whatever stage and knowing that my beauty does not lie within my hair. It lies within the many qualities and attributes that I obtain. Making these hairpieces and spending time with my hair has been cathartic, an exploration of the wonders of what my hair can do, and the inspiration it will serve to many. My hair is beautiful and so magical. Learning about my hair brings me closer within myself and makes me feel grounded. This is a relationship with myself that can only grow stronger.

Halina Edwards.
Freelance designer and researcher.

Halina currently works as Lead Designer at The Black Curriculum, leading on projects such as the TBC Zine and overseeing art direction of learning resources. Since completing her MA at the University of Westminster studying Menswear Design, she has produced designs under her own name, Flock Together and Ganni, also conducting research for director Akinola Davies Jr.

Sheda,
of Holda Poetry

POET

1 of 100 Voices Still Breathing

Flashback.

She was in my face, I stood stock still in white knee-high socks. I know I knew the answer, then I didn't. It was easy – three times three times three.

My three times table, I had the star. She took away 'My Gold Star' on the grid.

From this young and impressionable age, I never forgot Mrs Duff.

Mrs Duff, my primary school teacher, was not nice to me.

No patience with me, it seemed she did not care I saw and felt it. In her class, she had a black girl, me; Mrs Duff may not have been too pleased. Mrs Duff you could have been nice, a better teacher for me instead of being so mean.

I learnt: teachers have power to do good.

Flashback.

Look, (bully) he gets away with bad words between his teeth.

Nig-nog, monkey and blackie, that's racial tension from somewhere, I heard it, it was the late '70s see.

The boy sputtered expletives, got highly

upset, irate and angry because as he chastised his sister, I walked past them on the way to school. I recall looking back with a smile, beguiled.

I learnt: 'Just because'. A phrase that would sometimes proceed before knowing me.

I can do this – still breathing.

Flashback.

As they lifted up their skirts, pulled down socks and tops to one side, to see what?

Years later I understood, it was a seasonal thing, mainly through the summer months.

Once the autumn months prevailed the 'tan' was gone, like most friendships fade.

Did we have anything in common?

Yes! When you fell in the playground, I saw your blood, so we're the same colour within.

I learnt: some people would like to have darker skin, like mine, I don't know why.

'I SAW YOUR BLOOD. SO WE'RE THE SAME COLOUR'

Here I am, among girlfriends at playtime, looking at them, showing each other the colour of their skin. Interesting?

They were so pleased it was darker, evident by the line which defined they had 'a tan'.

That's what they called it when you 'caught the sun'.

For measure they would put their skin against mine. Why?

What they said, let us not replay, let's carry on.

Sheda.
Poet.

Sheda writes under the pen name of 'Holda Poetry'. She is the founder of Poets and Monologues, a bimonthly event featuring established and new poets. Most recently, she performed her first reading at the *Financial Times* Oxford Literary Festival and had her first photographic poetic exhibition.

Trish Cooke

PLAYWRIGHT, ACTOR, TELEVISION PRESENTER, SCRIPTWRITER AND CHILDREN'S AUTHOR

First Encounters with Racism

As a kid, growing up on a council estate in Bradford, there were enough times I was called 'wog' and many other derogatory names that the white kids dared to throw at me. But somehow, I could handle that. I mean, I gave as good as I got . . . kinda. Though I must admit, the words my big sister advised I should use felt somewhat inadequate.

The phrase 'white trash' never quite stood up to the ugly words they called me. For a start, I didn't fully understand what the phrase meant. No one from where I lived used the word 'trash'. It was an American term and so it did not come easily from my tongue and I felt a bit posh and up myself. Still when that curly-haired scruff from up the road slung those names at me, I felt an air of superiority belting out 'White trash!' at the top of my voice, and looking at his puzzled expression, as he tried to work out what it meant, never failed to amuse me. I think the fact that I had seven older siblings meant that, other than name-calling, growing up no one really ever messed with me.

Looking back, I don't think the name-calling was the most hurtful thing that happened. There was always a niggling feeling that I couldn't quite understand and that was caused, surprisingly, by how my white friends handled the name-calling. When they stood up for me, they would say things like, 'It's not her fault. She was born like that!' or 'She's not like the other ones. She's just like us really.'

Their words were supposed to make me feel better, but they didn't. The underlying message I was getting from them was that I was inferior, but it wasn't my fault.

IT TRIGGERED A LOT OF
QUESTIONS

I remember the first time I felt direct racism. I mean, blatant, to my face. Worse than name-calling because I had nothing to throw back and I didn't know what to do about it. I think I must have been about seven or eight at the time.

My friend, who lived next door, asked me to join the Brownies with her. Jane (for the sake of this article), an older girl, who lived further down our street, had invited her. Jane was the Brown Owl and in charge of the meetings. I was so excited. I had regularly seen Jane lead the neighbourhood kids, like the Pied Piper, down the street, as they went to Brownies every week and I couldn't wait to join them. So, when Jane called to get my friend, I tagged along and went to the first introductory session. When I got home, I was still buzzing. I told my mum I needed to get the uniform and, though pushed for cash, Mum was on board to get me kitted out.

The next day Jane came knocking on our door and in a hushed, apologetic voice I heard her telling Mum how she didn't think it would be a good idea for me to come to any more of the Brownie sessions, as coloured children weren't allowed. I remember my mum cursing her in French creole as she left, tail between her legs. It was a cruel awakening of what the world was like. It triggered a lot of questions inside me.

Trish Cooke.
Playwright, actor, television presenter, scriptwriter and children's author.

Among her many accolades, Trish has been awarded for her theatre writing and her panto, *Rapunzel*, was nominated for an Olivier Award. She has written extensively for BBC Radio. Her children's book, *So Much*, is critically acclaimed and was voted one of the 100 best children's books by *Time Out* in 2016.

Jocelyn Jee Esien

COMEDIAN, ACTOR AND WRITER

It's Time

A LIFETIME of being told it's not when I know it is

YEARS of my feelings pushed to the back of the queue behind hers and his

CONSTANTLY needing and choosing to share my pain

To ALWAYS have it then turned against me into blame.

EVERY SO OFTEN being called up to fill the 'Tell me what it's like' slot

TIME AFTER TIME feeling forced to talk about something I'd rather not

OCCASIONALLY making sure I pick the right words

So I NEVER make the listener feel hurt

NOW I thank God for resilience and my black-don't-crack tough skin

THESE DAYS I look back on all those past days as a win

TODAY I walk strong, knowing and loud

Because I'll FOREVER be black, powerful and proud

Jocelyn Jee Esien.
Comedian, actor and writer.

Jocelyn stars in the hidden-camera show, *3 Non-Blondes*. She is the first black woman to have her own television comedy sketch show, *Little Miss Jocelyn*.

I'LL FOREVER BE BLACK, POWERFUL & PROUD

Sharon
Walters

ARTIST

S

Racism is not always overt. It can be a series of episodes or unspoken subtexts that have had the most impact. The subtleties that are cleverly disguised behind comments, behind looks, or mentions of expectations of what people like me 'like'. It has been the school staff member who comes down to greet the education consultant at reception, calls out my name but refuses to look at me, as surely someone of that status could not be me. After all, I am black.

I HAD NO CHOICE BUT TO SIT WITH

MY EMOTIONS

AND PROCESS THEM

The heady and sickening mix of yet another black body slain on our screens through the murder of George Floyd, when already living through a global pandemic, triggered memories of the many instances of racism I had been subjected to. For so long, I had felt the need to box those experiences up; it was simply too painful to lift the lid and peek inside. Like many of us, Lockdown 2020 took me from my usual routine. When on furlough I had time to reflect. The lid of those difficult experiences had been lifted and they came cascading out. I had no choice but to sit with my emotions and process them. **>**

Over time, the experiences gradually began to wear me down unknowingly. In 2018, I started the *Seeing Ourselves* collage series. It began as a direct response to the lack of visibility of black women in several arenas, including arts and heritage, and mainstream Western media. I wanted to create work to celebrate black women, I wanted us to be *seen* and as the series progressed, I realized it became increasingly important to be *heard* too.

Every one of the more than 250 collages reaffirms my right to 'take up space'; the work is a meditation on empowerment. *Wakanda* is the signature piece of the series, inspired by the *Black Panther* movie. She depicts strength, power, and determination; a celebration of her natural beauty with no need to conform to Western definitions of beauty.

The collage series is an extension of the community engagement collaboration work I have done for many years. It is my attempt to have a voice for myself and others like me. For all those times people have turned a blind eye to blatant discrimination, or made 'jokes' based on race, or not heard my voice.

I have now made the decision to step away from the environments where I am not valued, where my opinions do not count on subjects other than race.

Enough is enough. It is time for me to stand up, and be seen and heard.

Sharon Walters.

Artist.

Sharon creates hand-assembled collages celebrating black women. The series entitled *Seeing Ourselves* explores underrepresentation in many arenas, particularly the arts, the heritage sector, and mainstream Western media. Her work was showcased in the ITV *Create* series, in which British artists were asked to interpret the channel's logo.

STAND UP, AND BE SEEN AND HEARD

Wakanda Artwork

Josephine
Melville

ACTOR, WRITER,
DIRECTOR AND
ARCHIVIST

Sending the Barrel Home

When I dwell on how racism has affected me over the years, I begin to feel a sense of rage and sadness that nobody has ever asked me to express it. Why would they? What good would that do?

If it does become a point of conversation, then I'm given the stock answers of, 'You're being oversensitive, it wasn't meant to hurt you', 'It's not racist, it's just how it is', 'I've got black friends, get over it', or 'You've got a chip on your shoulder'.

My parents would say, life is not easy, you got to have a thick skin and be 100 times better than your friends. Study harder, work harder, shut up, put a lid on it. On all those feelings, put the lid on it and send the barrel home!

When my parents came to London in the 1950s, they were seeking a better life. My mum and dad, Beryl and Edwin Melville, met in east London at a party, one of the weekly gatherings to drink, dance, and play dominoes. They met, fell in love, and started a family – my family. They wanted to give us a better life, here in the mother country. The land of milk and honey, where the streets were paved with gold. But they weren't paved with gold; they were paved with hostility, rejection, and bad mind! So, my parents had to prepare us for what was to come.

One of my fondest memories was when they used to buy a big barrel to send back to family in Jamaica. They would stock it with staple supplies, like rice, oil, toiletries, and clothes. Stuffing and filling the barrel, trying to be positive.

But it was like they were locking away the hurt and pain and unsatisfied feelings, of what the real situation was here in London. However, I saw it as a time of excitement and I would help to fill the barrel, putting in my old toys and clothes that didn't fit, even though I didn't realize at the time that I was also putting in my memories that I chose to ignore and didn't need. Put them all in the barrel, push them down, deep down, and send them home!

Close the lid on feelings of disappointment, memories of the only black girl studying ballroom dancing before *Strictly Come Dancing* was even a thing, and not being able to enter competitions, because I would have to have a male partner and none of the white boys wanted to dance with me, because I was black.

Pursuing my career, performing in a show in Manchester and standing in a pillar-box-red phone box, on the phone to my dad, having the door pulled open, as somebody would hurl abuse, saying, 'Nigger, get out! Go back to your own country!'

How brave my parents must have been coming to England and moving like warriors, like athletes during that time, passing that baton on to us. That baton of bravery and resilience, determination and fight, and spirit and faith, hoping that by the time I grew up I would be prepared for what was to come, or that things would have changed for the better.

We don't send barrels home any more. They resorted to just sending money when they could. However, in the lean-to shed my dad built as the DIY extension on the house, there was still one barrel left in the corner. It never got sent. The last barrel stocked with things pushed deep down. My dad said before he died that this last barrel was for emergencies if times got hard. Stocked with things for just in case: hidden feelings and memories. For just in case, with the lid tightly fastened.

I have decided to open the barrel, to take the lid off. It's time to write a new story, because this is my home and what I pass on to my children won't be a locked barrel of regret, but the baton of empowerment and strength of character to change the uncomfortable truths, and live a life out of the barrel, to carry on our family legacy.

Josephine Melville.
Actor, writer, director and archivist.
Josephine is the founder of the South Essex African Caribbean Association, a founder member of the BiBi Crew, and a cofounder member of Aarawak Moon Productions. Josephine cowrote the play *Shoot to Win*, which has been performed in the UK and the USA.

Rakie
Ayola

ACTOR AND WRITER

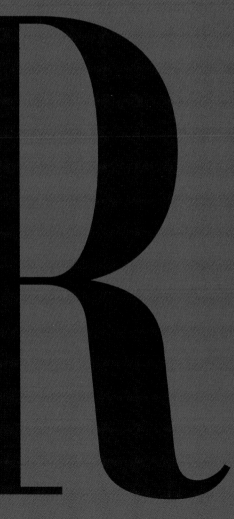

Consequences

Six people walking down a street. Two teenage girls in front. Two pre-teen boys behind. On the other side of the road heading in the same direction, a 3-year-old girl and me. An adult. The only one of them known to me is the 3-year-old. I'm holding her hand. She's my friend's daughter. It's a beautiful day and I'm taking her for a walk around the leafy neighbourhood.

From across the road, I hear that word.

Like a large unwieldy stone, awkward and heavy, it manages to make contact with both my head and my heart. I reel internally, but keep walking. The 3 year old is saying something about her shoes. As she witters on I try to remember the last time I was called that word.

I realize this is the *first* time I've been called that word.

My reaction springs from an emotional connection to it that runs deep. A connection that began the moment I saw its corrosive effect on others and felt the venom with which it's used.

A boy of 9 or 10 has just hurled that word at me like a hand grenade and he's walking away unscathed. And I'm walking away. Wounded.

Suddenly I stop. I cross the road. The 3-year-old asks where we're going.

'To talk to those boys,' I say.

The girls are still ahead. Oblivious.

The 3-year-old and I reach the pavement in front of the boys. They stop and peer up at me. I stop and stare down at them.

'Do I know you?'

Eyes huge, they shake their heads.

'Do you know me?'

They mumble, 'No.'

I take them in. These children. I find myself wondering what circumstances led to this moment. I wonder what these boys have seen and heard and been taught that made hurling that word any kind of option. I wonder if they know its effect. I wonder if they care. I'm a grown-up: why the fuck don't they care?

I bend closer. Narrow my eyes. Reduce my voice to a low whisper.

'I could be your new neighbour . . .

'I could be your next teacher . . .

'I could be your dentist.'

I realize they're trembling. Terrified.

I realize I'm glad.

'What's going on?'

The teenage girls have noticed the boys are talking to a stranger.

With my eyes still on the boys, I say, 'I'll leave them to tell you.'

'This is boring,' says the 3-year-old.

'Yes, it is,' I say. We turn and walk away.

I look back in time to see one of the girls slapping one of the boys across the head. He cries out in pain. I watch as he sobs.

I blink as my eyes burn.

'I'm tired,' whines the 3-year-old.

'So am I,' I say. 'So am I.'

I lift her onto my back and walk on.

Rakie Ayola.
Actor and writer.

Rakie is best known for playing Kyla Tyson in BBC's *Holby City*, and Hermione Granger in the West End production of *Harry Potter and the Cursed Child*. She is a Fellow of the Royal Welsh College of Music and Drama, and cofounded Shanty Productions, which produced the short film *Persephone's Playground*.

I REALIZE, THIS IS THE FIRST TIME I'VE BEEN CALLED THAT

THAT WORD

Errol
Donald

ARTIST, DESIGNER,
WRITER, WELLNESS
COACH, AND FOUNDER
OF MINDSPRAY
ASSOCIATES

E

Errol Donald, aka 'Pride'.

Errol Donald.

Artist, designer, writer, wellness coach, and founder of Mindspray Associates.

Errol is a qualified child therapist, wellbeing practitioner, and the founder and director of Mindspray. He is acknowledged as a leading figure within the development of British graffiti art. Errol has worked extensively in community settings where he observes creative, intercultural practice with an awareness of the cognitive, emotional, and educational needs of young people.

Veronica McKenzie

FILM-MAKER, WRITER, DIRECTOR AND PRODUCER

The Silence

It was 1997. I remember because it was the year Princess Diana died. It was also the first time I thought about getting out of bed and driving into work at 3 a.m. I had heard the news about her death on LBC, a talk radio show that barely anyone listened to back then. I was always interested in other people's opinions of the news: whether it was Beryl from Bermondsey with her muddled and comical calls, or the lady from Finchley, who managed to lob in a smutty innuendo on every topic, I was addicted.

I called my mate Sandra. She thought I was talking about Diana in Trinidad, a mutual friend. 'Not *that* Diana,' I said. '*Our* Diana.' Because it felt like Diana was ours – black, white, old, or young. We all mourned together when she died. It didn't get more British than that.

I thought of myself, when filling in the box on a form as 'Black British'. Proud to be of Jamaican descent, and Tottenham through and through. My colleagues at L!ve TV, were mostly younger, very privileged, and generally nice. We worked damn hard. Even though the station wasn't seen as a respectable channel, it was highly inventive. We had a pink news bunny!

We had a woman reading stock market tips while stripping. We actually mulled over an idea for a show called *Weighing the Fat Man*, where you would – like in a fairground – get a fat man on the scales and see how many Maltesers he weighed. It didn't get commissioned; probably pipped by twins doing the weather. I mention this to point out that it wasn't a politically correct workplace. It was fast, crazy, and I loved it.

BECAUSE IT FELT LIKE DIANA WAS OURS

BLACK, WHITE OLD OR YOUNG.

WE ALL MOURNED TOGETHER WHEN SHE DIED

Starting as an intern, I was one of the few that had been given a proper job, and was just so happy to be working 'in TV' that I didn't quibble about the extremely low pay. From being a researcher on a pet show, I moved to doing makeovers, formats that are popular today, but back then were seen as tacky. I lapped it up.

One incident stands out. I had been at L!ve for almost a year, settling in fairly well, enjoying after-work drinks at the fancy bars in Canary Wharf, invited to cool restaurant openings, living the London life! **>**

One day I was in the toilets, fixing my dress. I worked hard to keep up a fashionista image on a budget.

Two colleagues came in and started talking. My name came up.

One said, 'Veronica is so nice'.

The other responded, 'Yes she's lovely'.

The first girl emphasized, 'She's just so nice.'

Then there was a long pause. I held my breath to hear what they said next. The silence went on for a long time, but it was probably only seconds. I felt with every fibre in my body what they were *not* saying. They were not saying, *for a black girl*. I don't know how I knew, but I knew. They carried on talking as I pushed the door open. Their red faces! I joked about my wonky dress and they relaxed. They were nice colleagues, but clearly surprised to click well with someone who was 'not one of them'. Someone different.

I went back to the main office and looked around properly, as if for the first time. There were perhaps 100 people. The fashion department with the very posh producer. The laddish news team. Forward planning. I looked for black faces. There were two. Of course, I had noticed them before. Though we worked in different sections, and sometimes had drinks with the group, we didn't band together. It's like we observed some unwritten rule when we joined up. Took on the mantra. *Everyone for themselves!* – somehow knowing it wouldn't be cool to meet up separately. Though nobody talked about race, I started paying attention to the unsaid. The silences. There was the black intern, who complained about racism and was let go the same day. The Asian

IT'S LIKE
WE OBSERVED
SOME

producer, who left having been bypassed for promotion. The homophobia. The women crying in the toilets. Fearful conversations in the smoking room. The senior manager jokily wondering how I had a Scottish surname, and me having to laugh along like *Oops! It just happened*. I saw that it was a toxic workplace, and that being desperate to work in TV meant many people were putting up with appalling treatment – me included. Soon after, I quit and never looked back.

'Though nobody talked about race, I started paying attention to the unsaid. The silences.'

VERONICA

UNWRITTEN RULE

Veronica McKenzie.
Film-maker, writer, director and producer.
Veronica set up Reel Brit Productions to produce uplifting, original, and entertaining stories, which often reframe popular culture. Her feature *Nine Nights* won the PAFF 2019 Narrative Feature Director Award.

Suzanne
Packer

ACTOR, TEACHER,
SINGER, AND
BROADCASTER

Stride Through and Past

The recent spotlight on racism in our lives churned me up. I felt empty and sad, traumatized and gutted, and worn out.

I hadn't realized how much I had ingested all this trauma until I was forced to look at the incidents of racism I had experienced.

My 'racism' has been the kind that eats away at your self-confidence. The kind that forces you to lower your expectations and believe that you will never be good enough to reach your potential.

THE KIND THAT FORCES YOU TO LOWER YOUR EXPECTATIONS

Starting with my grandfather, my family came over from Jamaica. I am 'lucky' not to have experienced the direct racism that my grandparents and parents were subject to when they first arrived in this country in the 1950s. I was also brought up in Wales, where I was unaware of being treated differently from the other children. However, I wasn't invited to certain birthday parties! Also, I watched as a bunch of lads in a minibus showed my family their arses when we were driving on the motorway, and a man spat at me when I was walking home from school. I think I just put them down as ignorant people doing ignorant things, and that they would probably have done these things to anyone. **>**

It never occurred to me that these were acts of racism, though my mum, who was a young woman at the time, in her thirties, remembers it differently. I know now. Interestingly, we never discussed it again until recently. I can see how my parents didn't want to burden us with this ugliness.

The 'subtlety' of racism came when I was at drama school. No provision in make-up class for my skin tone. I was going to leave before the end of term, as I had been offered a job which came with an Equity card. Equity cards were hard to come by back then. So, there was no way I was going to miss this chance. I was called in to see the Head of Acting, I now realize, for my 'graduation' speech.

On congratulating me on nailing the audition, I was 'advised' to get used to being unemployed because of my colour. They may not have been the exact words, but there was the message, loud and clear: Your colour will bar you from regular employment. My colour. Not my talent. My colour.

It's odd, but it's only since the murder of George Floyd and the response of the Black Lives Matter movement that I have allowed myself to remember how I felt when I heard that.

As I sat on my living room floor in 2020, thirty-five years after that *chat*, and as a successful actor, I gave myself the time to feel the gut-wrenching disappointment and hopelessness I had felt at the time. What was that message? It doesn't matter how hard I worked, how much I invested in time, money, and commitment in the industry I had chosen to forge a career in. None of that would matter. Because I am black.

Yes, I was crushed, and my ambition at

EVEN NOW THE MESSAGE IS THAT THEIR TALENT WILL NOT HAVE THE SAME OPPORTUNITIES TO FLOURISH

that time. But not for long. I didn't realize it then, but it gave me the push to become more skilled at what I do and to work even harder.

In fact, I became so determined to always be employed that I chose to become a teacher eventually, as well as an actor, and a singer, and a director, and a presenter – She who laughs last . . . !

Becoming a teacher has been as rewarding as being a performer. I am so aware of the messages that young black actors receive every time they watch the TV and go to the theatre. Even now the message is that their talent will not have the same opportunities to flourish and develop because they are black. My job is to encourage them to *not* be distracted by these negative messages and to 'stay focused on becoming the unique performers that you are'.

Even when I feel downhearted, I know I must use my voice and privileged platform to encourage the youth that are coming behind me. I have one of my own and I won't have his spirit crushed the way mine was.

So, I am determined to *stride through and past* all the other racist stories I hold.

With purpose.

Suzanne Packer.
Actor, teacher, singer, and broadcaster.

Suzanne is best known for her roles on TV, in *Brookside* and *Casualty*. She is equally at home in the classroom, having trained as a teacher in 1996. She is a Senior Lecturer in Acting at the Royal Welsh College of Music and Drama, in Cardiff; a founder member of the BiBi Crew; and great friends with her co-author, Suzette Llewellyn.

AND

DEVELOP

BECAUSE THEY ARE BLACK

Mzz Kimberley

ACTOR, SINGER AND
TRANS ACTIVIST

Pride and Strength

Growing up in the 1980s I never really questioned racism. Being black, light-skinned, with hazel eyes and smooth hair in a predominantly white school and neighbourhood made me more accepted by white people. I did not really understand that at the time.

There was this horrible boy who always called me 'the popular black kid'. I thought that was because I was into theatre and in the choir. My memories are painful. I remember in swimming class, white boys laughed at another black kid because when he got out of the pool his hair didn't move. How they would talk in front of me about other black people: 'Her lips are too big', or 'Black girls have big arses'. Funny how things turn out, with so many white girls now wanting big lips and a big ass.

I had a beautiful dark-skinned friend, Elsia. She was so beautiful. She upset the white girls by being beautiful; a goddess who took your breath away. The only thing they could say about her was, 'She's too dark'. How pathetic.

As I have grown into an adult with my own mind, I now realize how racism is a huge part of life and have come to understand that it's not only about hate. Racism is buried deep within until it becomes normalized. Most do not even know the true definition of racism, or realize their hurtful actions are racist. Many in our community have had their own experiences, some worse than others.

I worked on the LGBT scene for many years and have been extremely successful. During that time I realized that having the backing of a powerful white man pushed me into areas many never got the chance to experience. I was the face of Heaven Nightclub, which was the most popular club in Europe and all white. However, I was still faced with racism.

I received racist hate mail, which the police told me had come from inside the club. One of the managers did not want me around. He did everything to discredit my name. In his head I was a bitch one day, rude the next, and full of myself the following day. He could not make up his mind why he actually hated me. He had a problem with a black trans woman calling the shots and bringing in the money which kept him employed. One night he got drunk and spat on me for no reason. I took it like a lady, but got my revenge not long after. He died and I turned up to his funeral in a huge black hat and veil, as the grieving widow, taking all the attention away from him as he lay there stiff. Payback is always a bitch.

I've reached the point where I don't want to be around white people who are ignorant of marginalized communities and use their privilege in unforgiving ways. White people who do not understand, or want to understand, the pain they have put us through have no place in my world. White people who say that slavery was a long time ago, and we should forget it and move on, make my blood boil. I'm never going to forget just to make them

feel more comfortable. And I will never forget the men and women who lived in the worst pain so I could have a better life. I will never ever disrespect their legacy. How dare you!

As I continue to walk on this planet, my eyes are open wider. When you are black, you always have to watch your back, you can't relax around certain Caucasians, because if there's a problem they will always stick together. Black people are always wrong and, of course white is always right. A racist could be your best friend, make love to you, share special moments with you, but keep you oppressed.

Sometimes I feel racists are jealous because we are special, in fashion, sport, singing, film, politics, as writers, etc. The first black American president is by far one of the most popular men in the world. He is handsome, intelligent, and won the Nobel Peace Prize. Black people are not supposed to be great, but we are, and these racists know it. We have had to fight hard and we will continue to stand up. No one can take our pride and strength away from us.

Even though the black community has had its share of challenges, it's made me strong, proud, and willing to keep fighting for social justice until my last breath of air.

Mzz Kimberley, aka 'Kim Tatum'.
Actor, singer and trans activist.

Born in America, but now living and working in London, Mzz Kimberley is the winner of the BOYZ award for best cabaret artist, and is the patron of CliniQ, a health service for the trans and non-binary community.

Judith
Jacob

ACTOR,
PRESENTER,
AND DJ

I Found my Voice

I have to say when I was younger, about twenty years ago, I never noticed when racial comments were made, either because of my naivety, or because I was just plain foolish. However, this has haunted me as I cannot change my lack of self-worth at that time.

I was 17 and working on a TV series about nurses, called *Angels*. The other regular cast members and I were at the producer's home. It was a hot day, and we were on her balcony. The conversation turned to *What is your fantasy?* I have no memory of what mine or any of the others' fantasies were, only that of the producer Julia Smith, who I must say, gave me that job and offered me the regular role of Carmel in *EastEnders*. She said her fantasy was to be in a hot country and be fanned by 'piccaninnies'. I was the only person of African descent sitting there and I remember the other cast members all looked at me. I said nothing. I felt it was an insult, otherwise why would my cast mates all look at me, but I did not work out why in my head. I came home and told the story to my family, who were in shock. I told it to my friends, who wanted to know what I'd said back.

Why did I not think it was wrong when I'd heard it? As an adult, and trying to analyse it now, I did not know enough about my culture and therefore did not have the confidence to challenge what I heard. I also think I wanted to be invisible.

However, the feeling of my stomach turning every time I remember that conversation has fuelled me to not allow myself to stew in silence. It has ensured that I will say something if I feel undermined, insulted because of my melanin.

In fact, on the set of *EastEnders*, a scene that I was not in had a character talking about the hand of the man playing my brother as if he was a monkey. (That is how I interpreted her lines.) I asked the actor playing my brother if he was happy with what was being said and if not, how far were we prepared to go – that is, were we prepared to lose our jobs? He said he would go as far as I wanted to go. I mentioned it to the producer, the same woman who had had the 'piccaninny' fantasy, that I found the line insulting and asked if it could be changed, which she did with no argument.

It has taken me a long time to find my voice, but I have found it.

Judith Jacob.

Actor, presenter, and DJ.

Judith is best known for her roles in *EastEnders*, *The Real McCoy*, and *No Problem*. She is a founder member of the BiBi Crew, and of the Black Theatre Coop. Judith produced and presented *Judith Jacob Yabba, Yabbas with Friends*, a live chat show with celebrity guests. She can be heard on Conscious Radio, hosting her own show.

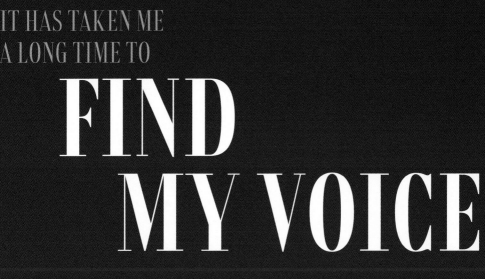

IT HAS TAKEN ME
A LONG TIME TO
FIND
MY VOICE

Josette
Bushell–
Mingo OBE

ACTRESS AND DIRECTOR

Ways I survive

It's an interesting question: 'How have you survived racism?' As if it's cancer or an affliction put deliberately upon someone, or it's so normal there is an accepted survival kit. And I suppose there is. I would like to ask white people how they survive racism, but that would be another book. As a child of working-class parents growing up in the East End of London I only knew diversity: my neighbours; my family, from Guyana, South America, uncles and cousins; friends at school; food; markets; old photo albums of my family back home; and sports.

But where I did not see diversity was on TV, in film, or in the theatre. Strange that I should find myself here today, as the Principle for Acting, at Stockholm University of the Arts. The first woman ever to hold the post and the first of African descent to sit in this position. Ever.

I have survived the terrible world of racism with one or two perspectives, as it is a constant battle to remain afloat, not be consumed, to find a way through, and create hope. I prefer to talk about survival and fucking up the odds rather than keep talking about what white people do.

My first way I survive is, in some ways, by mistake. The career I led as a black - British actress was without borders; that is, I auditioned; I got the part. It's hard to explain, but I never learnt that I could not do something in my career: I played Juliet, Elvis Presley, a crow in *Snow White*, a queen in *Measure for Measure*, Sylvia in *The Two Gentlemen of Verona* at the RSC, and Crooks in *Of Mice and Men*, staged by Complicite Theatre Company and the National Theatre Company; I played Cassandra and Cleopatra, all of the women in *Peer Gynt*, and Rafiki the lion in *The Lion King . . .* and that's just part of my career.

The mistake, the accident, is that I just did not expect and did not stand for it. That racism thing. It just was not possible. I just managed to play these roles. Using this book's title as a metaphor, I learnt to breathe underwater and the deeper I went, the more I could see.

The second way I survived is perspective. That is, I understood what had happened to us as African; decent people stolen from Africa; sold as property, subjected to the most horrific life of servitude, murder, rape; reduced to less than animals; the legacy of that today across the world. *This* is my greatest survival kit. I carry it with me. I unpack it when I am lost. I examine it when I am afraid. I look at my history's/herstory's story and I realize I am here. Nothing, no one will ever buy my freedom.

I also survive because the fear of doing nothing is greater than death. By learning and educating, and releasing in me the gods, goddesses, kings, and queens, the global black diaspora of myself, the millions upon >

THIS IS MY GREATEST

SURVIVAL

KIT

millions of shoulders on which I stand. The blackness that absorbs all things, that I am descended from – greatness. I learn about our beauty and grace, and community, arts, and culture as African-descent people, and my Northern Star becomes clear and I realize I am here. Nothing, no one will buy my freedom ever again.

Another way I survive is because I see myself on the great continuum. If I can be of service to my people, through my art, then I will be of service to all. So, I created the National Black Theatre of Sweden, which I hope, one day, will be a Northern Star for others. As Maya Angelou declared in her great poem, 'And Still I Rise', everything I am today is 'the hope and the dream of the slave'.

And this poem is mine:

This will not remain
I know that we are looking
From high,
A little unstable at times
On those shoulders
But from that height
When I look
Really look
I see us
Breathing, flying, singing, walking
And then I step into the great line
The seven rivers as Uncle Okri called it
And in that flow
Through pain, and George, and my life that matters
I am fearless

THE BLACKNESS
THAT ABSORBS ALL THINGS, THAT I AM DESCENDED
FROM

My rage heating me like Marvel comic hero

Wakanda for ever, for always

By any means necessary will I lift us up

So we can see into the mirror of our gods and princes

And if fear

Comes, as it must, gnawing at my bones

I look at the white soldier sitting on the shoulders of a small black boy

Using him as a stool in the hot African jungle

and he cannot breathe, so I must breathe for him

and I watch hope walk away because it has understood it is a mirage, a chimera that cannot sustain –

'I am the hope and the dream of the slave,' said my Auntie Maya

So, every day is my day, every day is my blackness

Every day I am perfect

No one
Nothing
Ever
Will take away my freedom
No one
Nothing
No one
No thing.

Josette Bushell-Mingo OBE.
Actress and director.

Josette was nominated for a Laurence Olivier Award for Best Actress in a Musical, for her role as Rafiki in *The Lion King*. She founded the black-led arts festival PUSH at the Young Vic. Josette was Associate Professor and Head of the Theatre Department at Stockholm University of the Arts. She will be the first person of African descent to be appointed Principal of the Royal Central School of Speech and Drama, a post she will take up at the start of the 2021-2 academic year.

GREATNESS

Michael Obiora

ACTOR, AUTHOR AND PRODUCER

Bursting the Bubble

On 9 May 2020, I became a first-time dad. The birth of my daughter increased the bubble in which I live. For two weeks I experienced an indescribable high.

On 25 May 2020, yet another unarmed black person was dehumanized and murdered by a white policeman. In the middle of the euphoria of welcoming our beautiful girl to the world, my bubble was deflating. The happiest period of my life, a time that had been a wonderful distraction from the global pandemic we found ourselves in, ran parallel to the rage that the killing of George Floyd sparked.

I'm sure I've always known this, but it's never been more clear to me than now that I create bubbles for myself as a defence mechanism. Whether it's me looking on the bright side after I've been stopped by the police for being black while driving – *Ultimately, they're jealous because I have a nice car. It's their problem*; or my 'operating from my higher self', when just about managing

not to respond to the micro-aggressions of being followed around a shop by security a little more closely than white patrons, or being told that I'm being aggressive if I raise a complaint of any sort, about anything; or whether the bubble I've created for myself was sparked by my white head of year telling the 11-year-old child-actor version of myself to 'Stop smiling. The cameras aren't rolling now. You in particular shouldn't feel you're any better than anybody else.' Oh well, she's an adult. She should know better. I'm living my dreams. Shame on her.

'You're articulate for a black person.'

'She's pretty for a black girl.'

'Things aren't as bad in the UK as they are in America.' Rashan Charles, Sean Rigg, Roger Sylvester, Joy Gardner, Cynthia Jarrett . . .

Etcetera, etcetera. Minimize, minimize. Suppress, suppress.

We all want to feel safe.

But now is not the time to put a plaster over wounds that need our attention until they heal once and for all. I almost never watch the news, I don't read the papers, and I almost never know what is trending. But I know that the world has finally had time over the past few months to notice what 'those guys' – us – mean when we say, 'Black lives matter.' This is not the time for Oppression Olympics. Now is not the time to counter the basic desire for equality with 'All lives matter'. It's time for white people to

be actively anti-racist. It's time for black and brown people to (continue to) support each other as we work through our trauma. We can all relate to trauma of some sort due to the fears we've had to navigate as the death toll from coronavirus spiked.

I've actually come out of my bubble to give my daughter her best chance at life as a black female. For the sake of all children and each other we must all fight silence. We must all empathize, and we must all be thankful for those who have gone before us in the fight for equality, for those who have done so, and continue to do so, out of selflessness, as opposed to wanting to be 'on trend'. If we miss this opportunity, it's on us.

Michael Obiora.

Actor, author and producer.

Michael is best known for his roles as Max Abassi in *Grange Hill*, Lloyd Asike in *Casualty*, and Ben Trueman in *Hotel Babylon*. He is the author of two novels, *Black Shoes* and *Vivian's Couch*.

Benedicta
Makeri

ARTIST

My name is Benedicta Makeri and growing up in east London, in the 1980s, I didn't enjoy school. I felt most happy when I could just find a space and read by myself, but I was constantly bullied and reluctant to confide in anyone for support for fear of further reprisals.

I had big ambitions for my future and wasn't afraid to try new things. My favourite subjects were Art and English. I never knew what I wanted to do when I left school and I thought I could be an artist, but I was never encouraged to make that a career. It was just my dream.

My life turned a corner when I started the process of joining the army, thinking it would give me some structure, but again I wasn't encouraged, and I felt like I was being brainwashed, so I decided to leave and take time out to travel the world.

It was as if things started to move very quickly and, coming back to London, I soon became the mother of two beautiful children. Life hasn't been easy and I want to protect my children as much as I can. When I was at college someone threw an egg at me because I was black, but the assailants drove off and I was left literally with egg on my face and a sadness in my heart.

I found my art again and am now realizing my dreams. My artistic name is Kicasso. I use my art as a therapy to help me through my troubled times and as a way of expressing myself. With everything that has happened recently, and the Black Lives Matter movement, I created a piece that I hope speaks for itself.

A SADNESS IN
MY HEART

Benedicta Makeri, aka 'Kicasso'.
Artist.

Stevie
Basaula

ACTOR, AUTHOR
AND PRODUCER

To be equal is what we want
To be free and loved
Just the same as you.
It's a beautiful thing that some of us may never know
Never to be excluded for our otherness
Our shade of skin
Never to be put down
Never to be bypassed because our names are a little more difficult to pronounce
Or our dark features are a little less palatable for your audiences.
They think we don't see it
But we do

IT'S A BEAUTIFUL THING THAT SOME OF US MAY NEVER KNOW

And it hurts.
But sometimes your treatment of me makes me stronger
It gives me the desire to be great, to be confident in my powers
In my skin and in my otherness.

Stevie Basaula.
Actor, author and producer.
Stevie is best known for his role as Isaac Baptiste in *Eastenders*. Before this he appeared in a number of stage plays including, *The Tempest*, *Romeo and Juliet*, *Whose Culture*, and *Takeaway*. He also appeared in the short film *Mandem*.

Beverley Knight MBE

SINGER AND ACTOR

Music, My Go-to Weapon of Choice

When I was at Cheltenham University, I was looking for accommodation – like every student. I saw a property, got on the phone to the landlady. She sounded perfectly pleasant. We arranged for me to visit the property. I remember it was an absolutely roasting hot day. I rang the bell. No one answered.

Eventually, a lady came to the door and said, 'Oh hello. Are you here for a viewing?'

I said, 'Yes, I'm Beverley Smith [which was my birth name]. I've come to see the property.'

She said, 'You know what . . . Mrs Long isn't here, but I'm sure she's just let the property, cos I saw her talking to another person. It sounded like they'd sealed the deal.'

'That's such a shame,' I said. 'But never mind.'

And I thanked her for the information and the heads-up and that was that.

It was a lovely hot day, so I went across the road to a corner shop to buy an ice lolly and got talking to a young woman there, as you do. She asked me if I was a student and I said yes. You know, polite conversation.

'I'm looking for somewhere to live,' I mentioned. 'I just missed out on a property.'

Mrs Long's name came up.

'Oh, I know Mrs Long,' she said.

As I was handing over my money for the ice lolly, the same woman who had just spoken to me at the house happened to walk by and the shop assistant pointed at her saying, 'There she is!'

That was Mrs Long all along? The same woman, who said I'd just missed Mrs Long and that the flat was already rented? You know when you're trying to just work it out in your mind? So, she had pretended to be someone else to stop me renting the flat? I'd never faced that kind of discrimination before. I checked with the young lady again to confirm I wasn't going crazy. That was something I thought was left in my parents' era, but here I was, decades on from when my parents had first arrived in the UK, facing exactly the same bullshit. I was shocked. I was hurt. I was angry.

My anger became fury when I went to the Student Union body and put in a complaint against her, citing what she'd done. They were completely and utterly indifferent. This was the reaction from a place that should have promoted critical thinking, and inclusivity, and acceptance. I was let down and disappointed. This was 1992, so I'd like to think that things have changed now.

I have a very high sense of my own self-worth, so racism, bigotry, and prejudice cannot, and will not, bring me down. My fightback was to be brilliant, quite frankly. I have a very wide circle of friends. They come from all creeds, faiths, races. People are people. If people are idiots, then they are idiots, not black idiots, white idiots, brown idiots, Muslim idiots, Jewish idiots. They are none of those. They are *idiots*. And that's how I go through my life. That's how I approach people.

I would say to a black child, 'Never stay silent. Hold your head high and *know* that you are just as good, if not better, than a lot of the people who are alongside you at university, and that as long as they have those prejudices and those mindsets, you are a better person. You are a better child. Never ever let this kind of attitude grind you down or make you think that you are less than.'

I believe that music is the international language of love. I believe music speaks truth to power, and I believe that you can break down many boundaries with music. That's always been my go-to weapon of choice. It's disarming. It's very hard to hate someone standing in front of you, singing powerfully with intent, with a smile, and with passion. It's hard to then face that person with hatred and with bigotry. Some do of course. Some will choose to, and that is up to them, but for me, that is always the way that I will rise, to paraphrase Dr Maya Angelou.

Beverley Knight MBE.
Singer and actor.

Beverley is an English recording artist and West End musical theatre star. She is one of the Leading Ladies, a British-American girl group consisting of 'leading ladies' from London's West End stage. Her soulful singing voice has led to the release of eight studio albums. Beverley is also an ambassador for many charities, including Christian Aid.

Suzette Llewellyn

ACTOR AND COMMUNICATION SUPPORT WORKER

I CRIED FOR THE

TEENAGE ME

AND THE HUMILIATION I'D FELT

Lighting the Touchpaper

In the midst of coronavirus mayhem, worsening news of sly and violent acts of racism, and protest marches, I received a WhatsApp message.

A WhatsApp message with a montage of beautiful African women to the soundtrack of Beyoncé's 'Brown Skin Girl'. The banner 'Being black is not a crime' came up on the screen.

I smiled broadly.

How beautiful, how cute, how . . . how . . . I began to cry, it seemed from nowhere, but it was clear it was from deep, deep within my psyche.

The WhatsApp message lit the touchpaper. I was crying for the five-year-old me, who had already known at that young age that the world thought her ugly because the world did not value her brown skin. The world did not think her skin was 'just like pearls', did not think her skin 'glowed like diamonds'.

I was crying for a world where brown girls feel compelled to bleach their skin to comply with the world's ideal of beauty – and that ideal is a white one.

And I cried big, fat, hot tears. Cried for the girl who at five felt the weight of racism, although she did not understand it. I cried for the girl who was never caught playing kiss chase because of her brown skin. I cried for the girl mocked daily by her primary school teacher for having a Welsh surname and a brown skin: 'The little Welsh girl, who isn't Welsh'. I cried for the teenage me, and the humiliation I'd felt as I was verbally abused and then punched in the face by a grown man on a Tube train filled with passengers.

And as I sat in that moment, crumpled and worn from crying, I felt overwhelmed and pessimistic. As I sat in that moment, I thought of all that had changed since the 1970s, when I was growing up, and all that hadn't. I thought of the many, many assaults on my character that I had survived despite living in a racist society. **>**

The many, many assaults I had survived! I thought of my Caribbean ancestors, who not only survived, but had created a rich culture out of the torture that was their world. It's been a long struggle.

I remembered my father's cousin putting a 'Free Angela Davies' poster up in our front-room window.

I remember how Linton Kwesi Johnson's poem, 'Sonny's Lettah', reverberated around our front room as it played on our stereo. How my parents, with Aunty Estelle and Uncle Vincent, nodded their heads and shared their tales of struggle in 1960s London.

I remember the chant, 'Thirteen dead and nothing said.'

I remember the Black People's Day of Action. I thought of the names that have been carried on banners in the fight for justice – the many, many names.

I am the daughter of survivors and I have thrived. I have thrived and I will not let the pain of racism soak up my joy.

I have taken strength from my family, my friends, and the wider pan-African community. They have helped me to know

I THOUGHT OF MY
CARIBBEAN
ANCESTORS

I am beautiful, and I am of value.

I played the WhatsApp clip again. And I thought of my daughters, my nephews, nieces.

I remembered the excited pride I felt when I first heard Bob and Marcia sing 'Young, Gifted and Black'. I smiled at the many anthems since; reminders of the beauty and power of my melanin.

It's been a long struggle.

Yes, brown skin girl, your back against the world, I would never trade you for anybody else.

Suzette Llewellyn.

Actor and communication support worker.

Suzette is best known for her roles as Sheree Trueman in *EastEnders*, Sister Cheryl Patching in *Surgical Spirit*, and Nanette Duval in *Holby City*. She is a trained sign-language communicator and has worked with Deafinitely Theatre. She is a founder member of the BiBi Crew, and great friends with her co-author, Suzanne Packer.

WHO NOT ONLY SURVIVED, BUT HAD CREATED A RICH CULTURE OUT OF THE TORTURE THAT WAS THEIR WORLD

Sistren

PODCASTERS, RADIO HOSTS
AND A CREATIVE COLLECTIVE

FEEL THAT POWER.

BELIEVE

AND SURRENDER TO IT

For the brown girls in every shade
of earth
    the heavens could find
Who were taught that they are nothing
but collateral damage, unwanted
goods, broken songs
of unstoppable longing –
It's time to reclaim what is yours.

You are not and will never
be constrained by the words
they use to define you.
Time to transform,
to dream,
to resist and rise
as you have always done.

Did you know, your story is a classic
tale of when a drop of faith and a pinch
of magic come together?
You are as infinite as the thousand
galaxies
    and ancient moons within you, waiting
    for you to stretch yourself
    in places you can shine.

Take up space.
You're rage and your fire
and your aches are divine.
Feel that power. Believe
and surrender to it.
It's your birthright.

If you're looking for God,
Look in the mirror.

Sistren.
Podcasters, radio hosts and a creative
collective.
    Sistren are laser-focused on telling stories
relevant to queer black women like them.
They started making podcasts in 2015.
They've run safen sex, toxic-love, and
self-empowerment workshops at colleges,
as well as hosting parties and teaching
poetry. Their need to amplify the voices
of black marginalized women and rebuild
their community meant the trio landed
on foundation.fm, an online station with
a zero-tolerance policy on racism, sexism,
homophobia, and transphobia.

Merissa
Hylton

SCULPTOR,
PAINTER,
POTTER AND
TEXTILE ARTIST

Imagine growing up as a black child in Britain, on the cusp of two societies: one where you're too black; and one where you're not black enough. That was my experience growing up on the outskirts of Reading, with my family being one of only two black families in the area.

As a young child, I was aware of my skin colour, hair texture, and features, but not aware of the differences it would make in my life. In the early 1980s, racism in the area I grew up in was covert, subtle, polite even. It was never seen or heard, but it was felt. It was the looks from suspicious shopkeepers, the steady dispersal of children as we entered the park or playground, the tone and treatment received from my teachers and the dinner ladies at school. I did, however, have a small group of friends with whom I felt safe and happy to play.

It wasn't until I was about the age of 9 or 10 that I realized that the ringleader of our friendship group was being raised by racist parents. The revelation came one day during the summer holidays when we were all playing outside, and she suggested that everyone went to her house to play. I was excited and ran to fetch my bike, at which point she turned around and said, 'Not you. You're not allowed.' When I asked why, she replied rather nonchalantly, 'My mum and dad said they don't want people like you in our house.'

The irony is this girl's mother had previously been our childminder. My brother and I had gone to their old house every day after school. Mind you, we had to sit on the floor, because we weren't allowed to sit on the sofas, we weren't allowed to use the upstairs bathroom, and we were only allowed to eat the (stale) biscuits that were in a particular tin. And this was the moment that racism really hit me. **>**

AS A YOUNG CHILD, I WAS AWARE OF MY

SKIN COLOR

Other instances throughout my childhood and into my teens only stood out later in life. Things such as my violin teacher scolding me after I had failed one of my grading exams, and telling me she didn't think the violin was 'the coloured child's choice of instrument anyway'. And a boy in secondary school tying his scarf around my neck and telling me he was going to lynch me.

Secondary school brought its own complications because it was a lot larger and a lot more diverse. The other black children would call me a 'coconut' and pick on me because of my choice of clothes and music (I was *really* into pop, punk, rock, funk, disco, etc.). I hadn't really listened to hip-hop, R&B, and so on, so I was kind of 'late to the party' in that regard. I was accused of trying to 'act white', and thinking I was better than the other black children. Add to that the fact that I was born with no fingers on one hand, due to Amniotic Band Syndrome, it meant I was an easy target. Needless to say, I changed my behaviour, appearance, and taste in music, just so I could fit in and catch a break.

Being a black child in a rural area presents its own unique experience of blackness. I had the safety of my home and my family, who were Jamaican and proud – my life definitely wasn't devoid of my heritage or culture. However, in my teens I realized that growing up where I did meant

I was never going to fit in with the groups of teens I tried to join from the inner-city areas or London. I was seen as not 'black enough', too 'soft', too 'country' to be part of the 'cool gang'.

And in the area where I grew up, I was just black. I wasn't 'one of them' and the subtle (and sometimes not so subtle) behaviour and attitudes towards me constantly reminded me of this.

As an adult, this is something I no longer tolerate. Yes, I am a black woman, but I'm not a monolith. I am a multilayered multidimensional being, and I no longer seek approval to be in a space. I celebrate my blackness, my culture, my heritage, and all the little quirks and nuances that make me who I am. If there's one thing growing up in this country has taught me, it's you're damned if you do and damned if you don't. Acceptance is subjective and I teach my children to embrace and celebrate their own individuality and diversity, as well as the individuality and diversity of others.

Merissa Hylton.
Sculptor, painter, potter and textile artist.

Merissa delights in working in clay. She founded the organization Black Visual Artists in 2017 to create a platform for black artists in the UK. She advocates strongly for art as a form of creative therapy to promote mental health and personal wellbeing.

'I teach my children to embrace and celebrate their own individuality and diversity'

Neequaye
'Dreph' Dsane

VISUAL ARTIST

My first experience of racism was in primary school in Slough. I'm not a strong swimmer and it's not something that I enjoy. I remember my teacher telling me that the reason I was struggling to get my 10-metre badge was that black people's bones were built differently, and that swimming was not something that came naturally to us. A couple of years later another teacher declined to put me in a class for extra support leading up to my eleven-plus. My parents took me out of that school and moved me to a comprehensive school in Windsor that didn't do the eleven-plus.

In the 1990s you could count the number of black families in Windsor on one hand. I never experienced overt racism. However, I now understand the impact of being called 'Velcro head', 'rubber lips', or even 'ugly' by one of my closest *friends*. I now understand the impact that would have on my self-image well into adulthood. I learnt early on that you could be black, but that blackness had to be palatable, and on white people's terms. A friend of mine who was of mixed heritage had lost his Nigerian father some years earlier. His white mother was not happy that he was spending a lot of time with my family. She told him that our family was 'not in the same league as theirs'.

When you are constantly in a room where you are the *other*, and being your authentic self is met with subtle resistance, you find ways to navigate that. My way was to sharpen my mind. Yes, the police stopped me regularly when I walked home late at night, but I prided myself on handling the police, as opposed to them handling me.

As a black man, I have learnt to navigate white women clutching their handbags as I walk down the escalator, them choosing to stand when the only empty seat on the train carriage is next to mine, or me being followed by the security guard every time I visit my local Tesco Express.

I never felt that I fitted in anywhere. It was the usual story of being too black, too white (whatever that means), too bumpkin (in London), or too African (before being African was cool). I searched for my tribe and travelled across the nation and abroad, only to find that my tribe of misfits was dotted across the globe.

Like many black fathers, mine told me I had to work twice as hard as my white counterparts to succeed. I realize now that, in part, that is the root of my all-or-nothing/excellence-only mindset, and I make no apologies for that.

Neequaye Dreph, aka 'Dreph'.
Visual artist.

'Dreph' is known for large-scale portraits and murals, often painted in the public sphere. His focus is on documenting the black-British experience and his work can be found worldwide. He is an illustration lecturer at Portsmouth University, and his work was showcased in the ITV *Create* series, in which British artists were asked to interpret the channel's logo.

Jacob
V. Joyce

MULTIDISCIPLINARY
ARTIST

Jacob V. Joyce.

Multidisciplinary artist.

Jacob is currently working as an illustrator for Global Justice, and creates artwork for international human rights campaigns, as well as comic books. He also performs as the front person for the band Screaming Toenail, which has close connections with The University of the Underground.

Lettie
Precious

PLAYWRIGHT, POET,
AUTHOR AND ARTIST

The Protest

He's a black young man, 19, skin dark, skin cocoa beans, melanin dances in his veins. Like his ancestors who perished on slave ships, and those who survived back lashings, ankle chains, knees on their necks, rape, rape, rape, he is thick-lipped, nappy-headed, no time for shape-ups. They call him Eli.

In front of his bathroom mirror, feet firmly planted in the small bathing room, a space decorated with a porcelain tub, toilet, and pink mats that say, 'Don't leave the toilet seat up', Eli stares at his young black body, slim, toned, and fit to tackle the world. In a five-foot-ten frame, he stands bare-chested, a white mask covering his mouth and nose. On it, the words, 'I can't breathe'. A black glove fits his right hand perfectly, leaving his knuckles exposed so he can make the perfect fist when he raises it in protest. Finally, the young man nestles a black beret, fixing it to the side. He's done his research: 'Power to the people'. He has one mission only today, and that is to go to the London protests and take justice into his own callused black hands, tired hands. He whispers, 'Dad's death wasn't in vain.' He takes his mother's lipstick and starts to scribble words on the cold mirror, his reflection blending with the blood red of the application. He reads his own words out loud as if to animate himself and start the engines, because really, he's never been this brave, this daring. So, he scribbles, letting his own words seep into his soul. They invigorate him.

Ring the alarm! Ring the alarm! There are black and brown bodies falling everywhere.

Ring the alarm! Ring the alarm! There are black and brown tears flooding the streets.

You don't need to close your eyes to hear screaming black voices clearly.

You don't have to be a master musician to hear black voices singing, 'Stop killing us!'

'Stop killing us!' From South Africa to Egypt, from France to Spain, from China to the Americas. **>**

BLACK VOICES SINGING
STOP KILLING US!

Black skin, black skin, don't rise black skin. Hearts breaking, heads spinning. Why us? why us?

Maybe we are supreme gods, maybe we are stronger than most, maybe we hide God under our melanin. You marvel at how you enslaved us, beat us, raped us, and yet we still stand strong. Maybe that's what scares you the most!

Golliwog this, golliwog that! Piccaninny! Piccaninny! Nigger this, nigger that! Now they shout it, scream it in broad daylight.

The UK police aren't innocent! I'm sick of this shit. The revolution must begin.

Eli becomes braver with each breath in Broomhill where he lives. A ghetto filled with Pakistanis and blacks; not a white face in sight unless they wear Adidas track bottoms, have more than five kids to get council housing and child tax credit, and line up at chemists for their methadone. South Yorkshire is still behind in more ways than one.

Across town, rundown old council flats, abandoned toys on balconies, hole-filled boxer shorts and t-shirts hang on makeshift clothing lines. A young man stands comfortably in his five-nine frame although he wishes it was more. Nineteen years in age, born in white skin, skin pale; the sun has given up trying to burn some colour into it. Hair blond, hair gelled, eyes the bluest shade of blue, with a mix of greys and deep-ocean blacks. He is what they call average build. They call him Canon.

Gleagless is his hometown, where lads in dark hoodies write 'Nigger' on doors, and 'LEAVE or ELSE'. Where eggs paint windows, yokes running down stained glass like the tears of those who get called 'Nigger this and nigger that'. He knows no different, so he laughs and high-fives his friend Tommy, his mate Mike, when they write 'Karen's a slag' on park swings and shag girls who are barely 13. That's how things are. They all know each other by name because their mums and dads went

THE UK POLICE AREN'T

INNOCENT!

I'M SICK OF THIS SHIT.

> *'The UK police aren't innocent!*
> *I'm sick of this shit. The revolution must begin.'*
>
> VERONICA

to school together, and so did their mums' mums and dads' dads. The Queen's Head is for Sunday dinners because Nan can't cook, and stepdad Patrick wants a pint or ten. At least Canon doesn't have to witness failed boxer fists rearrange his mother Linda's cheekbones, leaving panda eyes on her pale face. No, not since Canon threatened to knock him out, because he's a man now.

Canon and John-that's his real dad-support Sheffield United. They've been going to every match since Canon was a boy, wearing the England colours on their faces and shouting at the top of their lungs how proud they are. Of course, tears have fallen when England have lost the World Cup time after time; Linda's worst days, because John wasn't any different from Patrick, only that he was a copper. They'd eat kebabs to dull the pain, or a curry, because that's the British thing to do, as was spending summers in Magaluf without knowing a single word in Spanish. That's the British thing to do. He loved his dad – well, *loves* him. He's not dead; he just left with a younger woman – fresh meat, fresh meat. Well, he wasn't dead before, but he's dead now, rumoured to have been killed by black boys yelling, 'No justice

no peace', for his alleged 'pig' crimes, a message left on his torso – 'Rest in hell you police scum'. Now Canon stands in fron of his bedroom mirror, feet planted firmly in the fading green carpet, skin dressed in tattoos from his knuckles to his chest and his arms, and of course, his neck, 'God first then an England flag with the date of his father's death. His mask covers his nose and thin lips, decorated with the snarling teeth of a rottweiler. Today he has one mission to go to the London protests to take justice into his own calloused white hands, raised in Methadone State! Nostrils flaring, hear pumping, to him, the revolution.

Lettie Precious.
Playwright, poet, author and artist.

In 2020 Lettie had pieces produced as par of the Royal Court's My White Friend online series, Theatre Royal Stratford East's audio project 8.46, Theatre 503 and Theatre Centre's ImagiNation audio visual project, and Jermyn Street Theatre's 15 Heroines. They won the 2019/2020 Royal Court and Kudos Fellowship. Their first full length play, This Is Us, is in development with Graeae Theatre.

Chinonyerem Odimba

PLAYWRIGHT, SCREENWRITER, POET, AND DIRECTOR

When I was born in Nigeria in the 1970s, I never guessed that my sense of beauty, belonging, and boldness would ever be questioned or completely denied. My 7-year-old self that found myself in the UK never guessed that my black skin would become a weapon that would be used against me. My father was a proud black man. My mother and her stream of sisters all extremely beautiful capable black women. Nothing prepared me for the rejection and heartache. I guess that experience of being pulled away from a place where I was not 'other', where in fact, I could be fully in my black-girl skin, became a trauma that I am still dealing with. That trauma transmuted into silence, defensiveness, and a shrinking that slowly tested my sense of who I was and who I could be.

In 2020, over thirty years since that black girl arrived at Heathrow airport, I was shocked to find some of those first odd feelings appearing again. Amid the collective grief, I was mourning that black girl. I was mourning a place where my otherness would disappear in a cloud of red dust and people with the same love for talking loudly.

THAT'S A THING OF BEAUTY TO SHARE

Being an artist, I cannot reach my stories without some access to my vulnerability. But my industry makes it clear that that vulnerability is not something it, or anyone recognizes in black girls or women. This is a painful path to walk. To tell stories is an honour I do not take lightly, but to tell stories in an industry that has very clear limits of what stories I should or I am allowed to tell sometimes feels like a heavy burden to carry.

The industry I want to work in doesn't just tolerate my stories, it celebrates them. It doesn't just try to understand why it is important to reflect black beauty, but makes sure that no black actress has to work with a make-up person who doesn't understand how to work with black skin. This industry will make me feel I belong by not just employing black people across the length and breadth of what it does, but also ensuring that its audiences understand that the stories we tell are just as eclectic and important as any other stories. To place the same value on plays by black writers as they have always done for plays by any other writer. And if we are really going to be bold in our new direction, then I want to be part of an industry that uses its imagination to have all the conversations we need to have, to make sure that the next black girl sees an acknowledgement of who she is – and the joy of that – constantly reflected back to her.

The daily fight to stay in your beauty, in your joy, in your power is something that feels so isolating and defeating sometimes, but I think that we can still find hope. We can find hope with each other. We can find hope in that change, however small, means something, and most importantly, as this year has shown; we can find some hope in that we are not alone in that fight.

My blackness is not an 'other'. It is utter joy, defiance, radical self-love. That's a thing of beauty to share.

Chinonyerem Odimba.
Playwright, screenwriter, poet, and director.
Chinonyerem was born in Nigeria and is currently Writer in Residence at the Royal Welsh College of Music and Drama in Cardiff, South Wales. Chinonyerem has been shortlisted for several writing awards, including the Alfred Fagon Award.

Treva Etienne

ACTOR, DIRECTOR AND FILM-MAKER

The Displaced People

The displaced people
Travel by day and by night
Trying to find a way to make
Their situation right.

Looking for answers why
The displaced people still wander
Thru life searching for a home
From London to Paris, from Paris to Rome.

The whole world needs to answer
The questions at hand
And all learn to listen to the problems and understand
Where do the displaced people really belong.
What did the displaced people ever do wrong?
It must have been something very strong
To still be paying the price

For something history still hasn't told
Us . . . Or has it?
Is it they who have it wrong and know it
But choose to deny?
Why would they lie?
Fear
Fear that lives with them daily
Fear that makes it mystery, myth
Total belief
Religion you could say – in a way
That if we – the displaced people – know our
True power
We will be the placed and they the displaced.

But until that mighty day happens
The displaced people
Travel by day and by night
Trying to find a way to make their situation right.

WHERE DO THE DISPLACED PEOPLE REALLY BELONG

Treva Etienne.
Actor, director and film-maker.

He works extensively in the USA, after a prolific career in the UK, on stage and on screen. Treva has written and directed two award-winning short films, *Driving Miss Crazy* and *A Woman Scorned*. He is currently coproducing a feature-length documentary on Archbishop Desmond Tutu and his message of global forgiveness.

Elliot Leachman

GRAPHIC DESIGNER

The Lioness at my Back

My experience, I feel, could have had a totally different outcome for me if I had had a different mother.

I was at the age at secondary school when I had to choose my subjects for Sixth Form.

This was very hard for me to do. I struggled with the thought of having to make important decisions for *my life* and my future. Wow!

This gave me many moody teenage moments. I simply didn't know exactly what my future or job prospects would be, other than I'd been told many times by teachers that I was excellent in all sports but not much else. Academically, I was all right. My grades were steady Cs, Bs and the odd A, but what I loved to do from an early age was doodle and draw things that I saw and I imagined (unknown to me, I was 3D sketching).

I turned to my mother for guidance. Truthfully, she insisted that we discussed at length the subjects I enjoyed and the hobbies I was best at.

With her help we placed my subject choices into an order which would help me map out a plan.

Graphics was one of my subjects, along with IT, which was different, and I was excited to further my knowledge. I also had an eye for photography.

Confidently, I handed in my chosen subjects and waited for my one-to-one with the teachers of my new subject classes. The day arrived for me to meet with my Graphics teacher. His name I will not mention, but he was, let me say, an unlikeable character; he was vain and loved to emasculate young boys, especially young black boys, who were a minority in my school. This is my truth.

I placed my hand out to greet him and he told me to take a seat. The vibe was set.

He wasted no time in asking me why I had chosen Graphics and I responded that Art and Graphics, the whole creativity, very much interested me. This I felt could lead me into the employment of marketing and branding.

I was then advised to choose another subject as, according to him, I would struggle with this subject and it would be a waste of his time and mine.

'Have you considered becoming a runner full-time, Elliot? You have a great talent there, boy.'

These words I will never ever forget, nor did I question the racism behind his sentence until I returned home deflated, degraded, and angry that he had made the confidence in me take a huge dive. I described to my mother what had been given to me as advice.

Well, shall I say the 'Lioness' in my mother surfaced with poise, strength, and an air of calm. My mum had my back. I overheard her request a face-to-face meeting with the Head and the Graphics teacher. I knew instantly this would not be good for him. My mother was already disappointed in the knowledge that he had not only ended his conversation with 'boy', but he had lazily stereotyped me, taking no responsibility as a teacher or as an adult with a certain duty of care for his students and their future. That the best I could achieve could only be in sport.

As I write this, I can honestly say the sense of pride and love I have for my mum now is even greater than that day.

As she insisted on me being present in that meeting, I witnessed my mother explain, with direction and clarity, that the ramifications of his words could have a damaging effect on my future. More importantly, if I had not had the support of a parent who could speak on my behalf and who believed in me, I would never have been given the tools to only believe in me, myself, and I.

After the meeting my mother made it clear that I would not be finishing my studies at that school. I would enrol in a college.

I was lucky to have met a great lecturer who after my interview walked me to my grandparents' car and told them how my portfolio outshone most of his final-year students, and that even though my application was late, I had been accepted.

After three years there, I then went on to London, then Cardiff Met University, and extended my course into a single honour's degree in Graphic Design with Communication.

Whether indirectly or directly, racism lives among us, and I know my intuition was correct regarding that teacher.

Elliot Leachman.
Graphic Designer.

Elliot recently graduated from Cardiff Met University with a BA Hons in Graphic Design and Communications. He describes setting up as a self-employed Graphic Designer as his proudest professional achievement so far.

Bumi Thomas

SINGER, SONGWRITER, PHOTOGRAPHER,
VISUAL COMMUNICATIONS ARTIST, AND ACTIVIST

My first breath was taken in Rutherglen, Glasgow, in the summer of 1983.

Since then, I have felt a close affinity with the land of my birth and my Nigerian heritage. Embracing the strands of my multiculturalism has always been a source of pride and an expression of the shared histories that inform my sense of identity. Scotland is the site of arrival in my story, the establishing shot.

Little did I know that, decades later, I would be forced to fight for my right to exist and go toe to toe with the British Government in the battle for my legitimacy, the right to live, work, love, and quite simply exist.

On 12 June 2019, I received a letter from the UK Home Office stating that my application for indefinite leave to remain had been refused and I had fourteen days to leave the country or face deportation – despite being born in the UK and having lived here for over twenty years. I was given the right to appeal. This was my only lifeline. With good counsel from my mentor, I found the courage to speak up about my experience, which led to incredible support.

Now was not the time to mourn the loss of my former life, although at times, it was so emotionally, psychologically, and physically overwhelming. It exposed the plight of Border Natives – people born in the UK, yet not recognized as citizens due to the 1981 British Nationality Act amendment – many of whom are still unaware of their status.

My life became a theatre with hecklers and enthusiasts alike. I was being called to abdicate the throne of my own sovereignty, find shards of my existence corroborated in other people's memories. My case became a cause célèbre, due to public outrage with the #JusticeforBumi petition that was signed by more than 25,000 people across England, Wales, Scotland, and Northern Ireland. The GoFundMe campaign I started got such a strong response that I was able to raise the funds for the best legal representation and fight the battle to the end.

On 23 October 2019, the High Court judge ruled in my favour, saying my deportation would not be in the interest of the British public, given my family ties, talent, and positive contribution to British Art and Culture. Despite this ruling, we had to litigate further through Judicial Review (JR), as the Home Office was keen to grant me limited leave to remain for thirty months, with the option to apply for settlement in 2023, with no guarantee of success. We fought this motion and were granted permission to move forward with the trial, at which point the Home Office conceded and agreed to settle out of court in April 2020.

I was awarded indefinite leave to remain (ILR) in August 2020. Bear in mind that, at this point, COVID-19 had brought the world to a complete standstill. In addition to the uncertainty, anxiety, and tension caused by the pandemic, there was this added layer of pressure causing inflammation to people, families, and communities caught in the cracks of the migratory system. >

EMBRACING
THE STRANDS OF MY MULTICULTURALISM HAS ALWAYS BEEN A SOURCE OF PRIDE

I learnt so much about the architecture of the soul. The fragility of identity, the whims of neo-imperialism, and the trans-ethnic consequence of neo-colonialism.

It was so hard to digest the logic that perpetuates this blend of inhumanity; a certain transactional cruelty directed at members of the Commonwealth states, citizens of former colonies, who in living memory, had the right and freedom to reside in the UK without restriction.

I think of the historical ties between Britain and the Commonwealth states; the post-war call in 1945 to help rebuild the nation; how the reconstruction of the British economy required a large influx of immigrant labour – in essence, a brain drain on these constituencies, which was then presented as a multilateral mutually beneficial arrangement between nations; how the Royal Commission on Population reported, in 1949, that immigrants of 'good stock' would be welcomed without reserve, due to the pressing needs of the labour market in the UK; the ongoing commodification of people of colour; and how this stance has devolved into the loss of freedom of movement through judiciary, parliamentary amendments and policy changes in 1962, 1968, 1971, 1974, 1981, and 1983, respectively. These changes continue to erode our sense of place, purpose, and value through these transatlantic movements, and I am overcome with a multitude of emotions, negotiating the complexities of human nature and counter-benevolence – specifically, the split personality of imperial Britain and humanitarian Britain, the power of political imagination for better or for worse, and the impact it has on the lives of so many tarred by the brush of this historical archetypical amnesia.

As I write this there is conflict within: one version of me is grappling with the injustice of this whole system of torture, extraction, and exclusion. The inner optimist whispers, 'Surely on some level there is room for interspecial, intergenerational resolve that rises above all forms of polarization, to attain a more evolved state of human consciousness?' Yet another part of me is unshakably clear on the socially and psychologically engineered instruments of oppression that perpetuate the archetype of the 'black' construct as less human, at home and abroad, and questions why we seem complicit in the auditing of our own essence.

In the aftermath of the ordeal, I am still raw. Yes, there are triggers. In popular-culture messaging, I see the confusion, criminality, the targeting of groups, weaponized xenophobia, threats of detention, threats of deportation, making it unbearable for the 'other' to live with dignity and the seduction of defeat served on a platter of exile.

I recognize the consequence as the contamination of innocence. You see, cynicism converts, converting what's left of our tenderness into hardened, callous husks regimented by the ritualistic demands of the insatiable ego. I find peace in the existence of a higher cause and higher power, in knowing that the suffering of one generation can become the fertilizer that will nourish the next, giving them the strength, tools, and insight to flourish powerfully.

I am here, still breathing

With my roots exposed, partially uprooted by the tension of uncertainty

Strained in the looming presence of judgement

I took refuge in the inner sanctum

Inner strength poured from the innately creative within,

The song 'Black child' was forged and it became my anthem.

Black child, child of the sun
Black child, no need to run
Black child, pearl of the sea
Black child, you were born free.

Bumi Thomas.
Singer, songwriter, photographer, visual communications artist, and activist.

Bumi was born in Glasgow, Scotland, but grew up in Nigeria. A law change, six months before she was born, affected the automatic citizenship rights of children born in the UK to parents from the Commonwealth. After a legal battle with the Home Office in 2019, Bumi was granted indefinite leave to remain in the UK.

WITH MY

ROOTS EXPOSED, PARTIALLY

UPROOTED

BY THE TENSION
OF UNCERTAINTY

Hand go, hand come.

BAHAMIAN PROVERB

Part II
Body, Mind and Soul

Beverley Michaels

Revd Dr Sharon Prentis

Ekow Suancheé

Dame Elizabeth Aniowu

Andrez Harriott

Busayo Twins

Jacqueline Antoine

Elis Jones

Dr Lorna Cork

Dr Robert Beckford

Carmen Smart

Dr Vanessa Apea

Revd Jide Macaulay

Nigel Walker

Teleica Kirkland

Fiona Compton

Maureen Nassoro

Sonia Obasogie

Dr Owen Williams

Beverley Randall

Colton Belgrave

Joyce Akpogheneta

Angela Jackson

Kai Harper

Yaw Amankona

Pamela Franklin

Bishop Rose

Michelle Griffith-Robinson

Dr Judith Agwada-Akeru

Tony Hendrickson

Beverley Michaels

HEADTEACHER AND THEATRE PRACTITIONER

Well, there I was at 13 with my sister, just past Dalston Lane and Hackney Downs Station in east London. A very different Hackney from what we know in 2020.

The 'Flats' group was diverse considering the time or decade we were in – the late 1970s. There were Greek Cypriots, white working-class British, Turkish Cypriots, black Caribbean and mixed race, African and white British males and females.

Hackney was the bed of immigrants settling and we were first generation, born in Britain amid the political climate of Enoch Powell, and so on.

We all stood side by side and on one occasion had each other's backs when the hostility grew between the boys and the Teds. We were being hunted down by a group of Teddy Boys wanting to get 'them'.

The clocks had just gone back, and we were all hanging around just opposite the pub where the Teds gathered and drank.

Regular banter occurred across Amherst Road, Dalston Lane, and Pembury Road crossroads.

We could be seen and heard. Their taunts were getting aggressive and the rebuttals were becoming threatening.

We heard glass crash suddenly and before we knew it, there they were, charging across.

We all scarpered in different directions, but the sisters stayed together, fear entering our hearts.

I wanted to cry, my heart was racing, and my breathing was struck with fear. I felt paralysed like you do when you find yourself running but going nowhere in a dream; your legs can't move because you are actually asleep. A stern rebuttal from my big sis brought me back to real time. 'Take them off!' she demanded as we ran for our lives into the estate where some of the group lived.

We lived off the main road further down. This place was our local but not our go-to safe spot, and we didn't have access to anyone's homes – we just hung out by the block, so we had to find safety somewhere. We ran looking over our shoulders and breathing as quietly as you can when you are running a 400-metre race! Up the stairs and on to the fourth floor, we crouched, and I then started to take out the Blakey's shoe protectors. My sis was not impressed.

We have been drafted in to become

'Never trouble trouble till trouble troubles you!'

JAMAICAN PROVERB THAT MEANS 'MIND YOUR OWN BUSINESS'

the participants of 'Find the niggers and skin them!'

Teds were known to be racist and due to the obvious *melanated* difference between us, the Greeks, and the Turks, we became targets. It was at this point we both started to pray for our lives: the Lord's Prayer.

We handed ourselves over to our ancestors.

Footsteps and grunts could be heard. We hardly drew breath for fear of the sound of our hearts beating louder out of our mouths. Big Sis put her hand over my mouth as tears started to well up in my eyes and my chest heaved to keep the breath still. She was stronger than me, had more anger in her, and yet here we were both vulnerable. If caught, we would have been abused or killed. We prayed hard and cried quietly to be saved by our ancestral angels.

For what seemed like an eternity we were up on the top floor crouching as low as we could, frozen in silence.

Let's move along the block until we get to the stairs, Big Sis signalled with her fingers. She moved and I followed as we crept and practically crawled our way out of the estate. We ran off into the night and went the long route home. A house. We couldn't get through our front door fast enough. The spirits of our ancestors let us free into the safety of our own home.

Did we go to the flats again? Hell, yeah!

Resilience reigned on our return. I vowed my future self would always provide opportunities to face the worst, as that night proved to be the worst-ever experience I have had in all my decades living as a black Briton.

My offspring are now storming the streets demanding equality and acknowledgement of BLM. I give thanks to those who paved the way for my generation. Racism will not prevail for our third generation born in the UK.

Coronavirus will not prevail as long as racism in Britain.

We will continue to breathe out loud!

Beverley Michaels.
Headteacher and theatre practitioner.

Beverley is a founder member of the BiBi Crew. As a former actor, she worked extensively in theatre and television, and starred in the seminal British film *Babylon*.

Revd Dr Sharon Prentis

It is one of the hardest roads a young child must travel, the journey of understanding, from innocence to the sobering reality that everyone is not regarded equally in society. I was 8 years old when I realized that I would not be treated in the same way as my white peers because of the colour of my skin. It was a bewildering insight for someone who, by nature, was curious, a voracious reader of anything she could get her hands on. What precipitated this revelation was my asking a question in class about a book I had read – *Uncle Tom's Cabin* by Harriet Beecher Stowe.

I wanted to know why the book was written, why the cruelty in it made me feel uncomfortable, and why we did not know more about the horrors of slavery. The questions became too much, and it was made known that this was not a suitable topic to pursue. I was crushed, isolated, and disempowered. The resultant sense of rejection hurt. It never occurred to me that the experiences of one character, Topsy, and my own originated from the same root cause: the oppression that comes from a society that does not fully acknowledge that bigotry and prejudice exist,

let alone prevents the conditions that allow them to flourish.

Up until then, I was completely oblivious to the fact that life was not fair. Owing to the careful efforts of my parents, the notion that I was not 'good enough' never really existed. As a curious child, I was an avid learner who asked questions with the expectation of receiving a response. My family had encouraged my desire to be curious about the world, so being dismissed and ignored was difficult. I stopped engaging because the psychological repercussions were too much! Even though I had that experience, it did not put me off reading. Instead, what it did was make me reluctant to ask or even answer questions in school. My curiosity went underground, along with my questions, which were only reserved for the occasional furtive whisper to friends.

When my parents noticed my withdrawal, they intuitively knew why and bought a second-hand set of the *Encyclopaedia Britannica*. They were yellowing, mildewed, and smelled musty because they were so old, but they were beautiful and a treasure chest of knowledge to me. Those reference books served as a source of information about the world and they revitalized my fading curiosity.

Following that experience, I learnt how easily our society normalizes elitism and supremacy by assuming that others are deficient; that we are educated to believe that all value is neutral and therefore fair, when in fact much of it is based on normative ideals of whiteness; that what you say and do is evaluated based on your race; that your credibility is questioned through statements such as 'You speak well' or 'Where were you born?'

When you are followed around a store, cast in the role of potential criminal. When your contribution is regarded as mundane at best, examined in greater scrutiny or, worse still, regurgitated only a few minutes later by your white colleagues even though you know you have just made that point. You make the choice between using your energy to resist, or to let it pass, knowing that you will need that energy for the work of healing. When you know that you must double your efforts, because your parents said you must work twice as hard to get half as far. When, later, you learn of the sadness you experience when you have to pass on that same wisdom to your own child.

In that final year of primary school, I became aware of racial and social injustice. However, there was also a wonderful teacher who not only encouraged me, but gave hope that there were some people who were willing to discuss difficult subjects and refute the attempts to silence black and brown people. That teacher is still etched on my memory.

Sometimes, I wonder just how much we have progressed. A poem by African-American priest, Pauli Murray, describes hope through difficult times as a song in the 'weary throat' of a brown girl. I identify with that. Despite the challenges, songs of hope illustrate a different future that I know will come. Until then, I will keep on singing.

The Revd Dr Sharon Prentis.
Sharon is Mission Enabler and Dean of Black and Minority Ethnic Affairs for the Church of England, in Birmingham. In 2003, her work was recognized by the Department of Health when she was named as a Mary Seacole Scholar for a project on faith and its impact on health.

Ekow Suancheé

ACTOR

A west- London kid, born with a West- African face, may sound poetic, but I can assure you this wasn't the case. My bubble, was predominantly white, but with a few South-Asian, Caribbean, and African families in sight. 'Don't stroke my dog. He'll attack. He doesn't like blacks.' My hope is that today's generation teaches old dogs new tricks.

I feel fortunate to now be able to love with my melanin-rich skin, even more considering the consensus that my parents, relatives, and ancestors' heritage was built upon savagery and cannibalism. I was asked continually where I was from; asked if I spoke African; why my palms were white; why my nose so big; and why was my skin so dark.

I watched my parents tone down their accents, traditions, talent, and truth, in order to placate the indigenous. Naturally I adopted this type of colonial, subservient behaviour, and as a teenager, embarking on a career as a professional sportsman, these tools did not stand me in good stead. In my twenties I carried resentment. My siblings and I are proud of our Manteo bloodline

and are also proud Londoners, – although when we were growing up, not all of society believed we belonged to this island.

I experienced horrific racism as a minor within this nation's most popular sport, at a time when it was not a criminal offence. The intrinsic superiority displayed by coaching staff and those of influence and power was far from covert. I was aware my skin, African features, and surname ignited the subconscious propaganda sequel, where they believed what they had been taught. This robbed me of self-love, confidence, direction, and belief, to be replaced by self-doubt, anxiety, cultural self-doubt, suppressed rage, and a distrust for white men in positions of power and influence.

The press, television, and literature made my physical make-up synonymous with laziness, a bad attitude, a lack of intelligence, aggression, anger, a lack of a father, poverty, lack of hygiene, sexual promiscuity, thieving, distrust, uncouthness, and animalistic traits.

A few black teammates of Caribbean origin within the club I was at as a teen would buy into the 'divide and rule' mentality. This happened in the 1990s. They were older than me and a bit lighter in complexion. The reference to my 'African darkness' was standard and regular. Colonialism created this narrative; alongside the Greater London school curriculum teachings about the amazing British Empire, Nazi Germany, and Communism; and the introduction of Black History Month in 1987, where pictures of dark-skinned men, women and children, lathered in petroleum jelly and chained together, filled the wall from the projector.

May I also state that a large majority of black Caribbean people know their true history and are proud of their African bloodline, roots, ancestors, and lineage.

I met many good-hearted people who were raised in 100- per- cent white communities.

people I deal with in other areas of my life, I keep in a place where the boundaries are taut, of which they are unaware – my way of protecting myself from potential triggers.

Today, I walk taller and prouder than ever. I celebrate my blemish-free, and vibrant skin, my Akan heritage and its customs – wealth, strength, and honour. I feel positive when I see that the younger generation know more about their ancestors' pre-enslavement history and have a sense of pride. The information age can piece together the parallels of the start of the Hundred Years' War in Europe with Mansa Musa's reign in sub-Saharan Africa, the Akans; or how Septimius Severus, who was a black, African Roman Emperor, ruled over Britain – we've always been here. Rochdale's cotton mill

MY SIBLINGS AND I ARE PROUD OF OUR
MANTEO BLOODLINE

We shared a dressing room. Teammates. Innocent fascination with my African roots was pleasant, but I always half-expected, or had an intuitive feeling, that an ignorant joke, innuendo, or comment might be spoken. I do believe there was no malice intended; it was the mere fact of trying too hard, by frequently returning to the subject of being black. To this day, I have retained a core group of friends in my circle, who I have known for many years, and they vary in their genetic make-up. The many other

workers, who refused to handle enslaved-grown cotton from the southern states, stood in solidarity with us.

May future generations of all races and complexions seek the truth of this nation, to ensure there will never be a repeat of this type of unfathomable human degradation.

Nyame Bless.

Ekow Suancheé.

Actor.

Ekow is a former footballer.

Dame Elizabeth Nneka Anionwu

RETIRED NURSE, AND CURRENT LECTURER AND EMERITUS PROFESSOR

'To be sure, the baby looks a little dark.'

These words were uttered in 1947 by a Catholic nun when my deeply religious maternal grandparents came to see my mother and me in the Mother and Baby Home in Birmingham. I was their first grandchild, but being brown wasn't to be the only stigma. My white mother was single and had been in her second year studying Classics at Cambridge University. When revealing that my (unnamed) father was a fellow student, she had omitted to mention that he was Nigerian.

I'm now 73 and have, thankfully, had a successful nursing career, despite numerous challenges thrown my way, many simply due to racism. My Irish-heritage grandparents, although incredibly shocked at the situation and insisting that my mother remain indoors during her pregnancy, had been supportive. Up until my birth they had originally hoped to avoid scandal from nosy neighbours by planning to claim me as their 'daughter' and enable my mother to continue her university studies. My arrival as a brown-skinned baby

with an Afro put an abrupt end to this idea!

My mother desperately wanted to provide a home for me and dropped out of university. Initially, she lived with her parents and took a secretarial course. I was placed 'temporarily' in a Catholic Children's Home and on the whole my nine years there were happy, but I have some vivid and negative experiences due to the colour of my skin. Here are some examples from my memoirs, *Mixed Blessings from a Cambridge Union*.

Washing my face ten times with soap to become white like my friends. I ended up in sick bay as I suffered from eczema and had very delicate skin.

Always wearing a cardigan in hot weather as I didn't want to show my brown arms.

Being proud that a nun had chosen me for the role of Humpty Dumpty in a show for all the children, then bawling my eyes out when another nun vetoed this as I was a 'half-caste'. You tell me, what on earth is the colour of Humpty Dumpty? To her eternal credit, the original nun argued forcibly and successfully in my favour. So, I was bursting with pride when my big scene arrived and the way, I fell off that wall was an Oscar-worthy performance. But I never forgot such racist cruelty meted out to such a young child.

At 9 I went to live with my mother and her husband. This only lasted for twenty months due to severe physical abuse at the hands of my stepfather, who could not cope with being teased at work for having – yep, here we go again – a 'half-caste' child in his home. I was rescued by my maternal grandparents and lived with them until the age of 16.

Then I applied to study to be a nurse at several London teaching hospitals. They all asked for a photograph of me, and the name and occupation of my father, which I didn't know. I do remember proudly listing my seven O levels. None of the hospitals replied! My devastation was overwhelming and I became confused and anxious about my future. Up until then, my upbringing had been totally among white people and, naively, I had no insight into the various manifestations of racism.

At the time I was working as a school nurse assistant, and the Medical Officer of Health, who clearly saw something in me, was incandescent with rage at the lack of responses. He signposted me to Paddington General Hospital, where I was accepted and duly qualified as a nurse in 1968.

Fast-forward a couple of years when I initially failed in my attempts to become a health visitor, even though I had passed all my written exams with flying colours. It was due to having challenged, during the required three months' practice placement, the illogical methods of collecting data on ethnic minorities, and also for pointing out the failure to use subsequently allocated funds appropriately. It was deemed by the local manager that I did not have the right 'attitude' to qualify. This judgement was speedily overturned when support came from activist friends, as by now I was becoming much more politically aware. The anger of such lived racism spurred me on to become involved in the field of health inequalities. In 1979 I proudly became the first sickle-cell nurse specialist in the UK.

Dame Elizabeth Nneka Anionwu. Retired nurse, and current lecturer and Emeritus Professor.

Dame Elizabeth Anionwu is currently a lecturer and Professor of Nursing at the University of West London, and was the first sickle cell and thalassaemia specialist nurse in Britain, and helped establish the Sickle Cell Society. Dame Elizabeth has written several books, including a bestselling memoir called *Mixed Blessings from a Cambridge Union*. She was presented with the Pride of Britain Lifetime Achievement Award in 2019, by pop star Janet Jackson.

Andrez Harriott

CEO AND MUSICIAN

Ten Times Harder

My mumma said, 'Son, you have to work ten times harder.' I didn't realize she was trying to protect me and make me stronger. It began with tiny little experiences which would confuse any child. Why did my friends' parents never invite me into their home? Why did the street that we lived on take an issue with us being in their space? Why did my teachers seem to look at some of me and my peers in this way?

In secondary school things began to make sense. They took Stephen Lawrence, and I knew that justice for children who looked like me was out of the question, even in death. We have never really recovered from this; it has underpinned too much of my work.

Music came along and provided me with life experiences, social mobility, and wider access. However, when you turn left on the plane and the other passengers give you that look – you know, the one that says, 'Where are you going?' – you are reminded of the bias which causes you silent stress.

There seemed to be an accepted narrative that no matter how far you climbed, the glass ceiling would always prevail. No matter how strong you were and no matter how far you pushed, there was something holding you back. It becomes exhausting!

2020 arrived and everything changed in 8 minutes and 46 seconds. Now we can talk, now we can begin to really understand the historical and intergenerational trauma that has long been overlooked. Many people in years to come will use this time to fill the history books. Organizations are trying to do the right thing, making small gestures, when what is really needed is a change to the structure.

I am stronger for the experiences, but I wish that the colour of my skin was not the first thing which defines how people engage with me. My friends and family of all ethnicities have become allies and in this I take much pride.

My ancestors', grandparents', and parents' generations had many challenges, but still they made a way for us.

Mumma said, 'Son, you have to work ten times harder.'

But to our daughter, we say, 'The world is now your oyster.'

IN THIS
I TAKE MUCH
PRIDE

Andrez Harriott, B.Sc., MA.
CEO and musician.

Andrez is the founder of the Liminality
Group. He has dedicated his life to working
with young people and young adults from
disadvantaged backgrounds at risk of
offending. In the 1990s, Andrez was part of
the British R&B band Damage, which sold
over 2 million records and toured the world.

Busayo Twins

POLICY AND VOICE DEVELOPMENT OFFICER

I was less than five minutes away from home, taking the same steps I always do, with the same careless strides I always take. I was about to cross the road when a car drew close to me, but didn't stop, just slowed down. I looked up, already envisioning myself on the other side accompanied with routine thoughts of my day and my plans for the rest of that evening. The night sky was making itself known, but not quite boldly enough to eclipse the sun. As my eyes flicked up, the car was passing by with the windows down. The back windows revealed at least two white men shouting and laughing as if they owned the car, as if they owned the roads.

The word 'monkey' left the vehicle. Maybe with other words or maybe alone. But the car did not stop; it accelerated as soon as it paralysed my body. I no longer saw myself across the road. I no longer thought about my evening or the familiarity of my surroundings. I didn't know where I was or where I was going. A breeze stroked my arms while my body waited for my lungs to breathe again. My eyes looked at the ghost of the car, reimagining a slowed-down version, in which I had time to anticipate what had

just happened. My mind immediately tried to reconstruct a version of events where I was in control, where I knew better. I looked around to see if anyone else had witnessed what I was struggling to piece together. There's never anyone around in London when these things happen, but the silence of the streets was deafening.

The caution of my parents came to fruition. These were no longer the occurrences of the past, a more ignorant time. It was today. In that moment I was reduced to my blackness. I felt my skin. My shadow took up space. My lips fuller than I remembered. I was invisible but out of place at the same time. My ears were ringing as if the men in the car were still slurring words about me. As if I could hear their dialogue from all the way back here. I imagined them laughing at me, dissecting every part of me. Then I considered whether they even remembered me at all. Maybe I was one of many people they had terrorized that day. Maybe I was so insignificant that by the next traffic light they had turned up the radio, slurped their beer, and spoken about the football. I don't even know which was worse: to be seen or forgotten.

I WAS STILL IN
ENRAGED
DISBELIEF

And even then, still on the same side of the road, still five minutes from my door, I wanted to explain myself. From confusion to shock to frustration, I wanted one thing – to speak. I wanted the opportunity they had robbed me of by driving past and not stopping. Even if I had 30 seconds to clarify: 'Who, me?' 'Excuse me?' Or 'F*ck you, you f*cking wallad!' But I remained still and relieved nobody saw this ridicule. So, in a weird way I was grateful that, in my emotional isolation, I'd been spared my dignity.

When it was clear that this was a reality that nobody could protect me from, I suddenly snapped back into the present. I chuckled like I was in control. To prove to myself that they were stupid people who were ignorant and belligerent. They didn't know me. I put one foot in front of the other and headed home. For those five minutes I was still in enraged disbelief. And although it wasn't my fault, I knew I wouldn't tell anyone what happened. The memory hid in the corners of my subconscious, only to resurface whenever anyone asked me, 'Have you ever actually experienced racism?'

Busayo Twins.
Policy and Voice Development Officer.

Busayo entered the reality television show *The Circle*, catfishing as a middle-class white male called Josh who, she thinks, will be the ultimate popular player. She is heavily involved in politics. She has appeared on the BBC and Victoria Derbyshire, and also shares her own views in Instagram stories.

MY MIND IMMEDIATELY TRIED TO
RECONSTRUCT

Jacqueline
Antoine

SWIMMING AND
AEROBICS INSTRUCTOR,
PERSONAL TRAINER,
AND MOTHER

Why Are There So Few Black Swimmers?

As a swimming teacher I am regularly asked why more black people don't swim. My answer is, it may not be simple, but the root is racism.

I was born in the UK to West- Indian parents; anti-black racism has been a presence, a hindrance, and a driving force throughout my life. It has taken me a while to realize the full scope of this.

As a schoolgirl in east London, it's not that I didn't experience racism, I just didn't know what it was. My parents taught me never to start a fight, but I didn't need to. Insults and fights found me, I was constantly defending myself and my family from attacks. However, it wasn't until I started in the workplace that I understood racism and recognized its impact on my life. The things that had been said to me when I was younger all made sense: from the disproportionate amount of West- Indian girls in the bottom sets for everything, to Sister Dubois, French teacher, clearly making it her life's mission to goad me into reacting until I was sent out of class. I loved and understood French innately, as do most West Indians who speak patois. I grew up thinking she had taken a personal dislike to me, but I realize I was one of many black students held back from excelling due to discrimination in education.

As a parent, I also taught my kids never to start a fight. However, I strived to ensure my children were prepared for the fight they would inevitably have to face. At the same time, I was still learning about the many levels of systemic racism at work in our lives. >

I UNDERSTOOD RACISM AND RECOGNIZED ITS IMPACT ON MY LIFE

MY CHILDREN WERE GIFTED AND I DEVOTED MY LIFE TO SUPPORTING THEIR POTENTIAL.

My children were gifted and I devoted my life to supporting their potential. This meant I was regularly introduced to new institutions: private school education, sports clubs, and so on. I began to recognize patterns of discrimination and discovered that vigilance and a constant presence (at a cost) were key to my children's success. Due to nepotism and favouritism in most clubs, associations, and committees, my constant presence was often not enough to prevent them from being blatantly overlooked. I think about the number of talented black children whose parents, due to work or another reason, weren't as available to provide encouragement, causing the children to lose interest and withdraw from a sometimes- hostile environment. The lack of representation is often unrelated to black children's aptitude and is more a reflection of the inherent discrimination within the institution.

I saw this with my own children – talented athletes who were regularly held back by club politics. So I became a cycling coach, a running coach, a football coach, a lifeguard, and a swimming teacher to try and infiltrate the network for the better of other marginalized children. I still question what these children could have become if given access to unbiased coaching and equal access to opportunities.

Through my role as a swimming teacher, it showed me that the leisure industry and UK sports as a whole is suffering an epidemic of inherent unchallenged racism.

Over twenty years, in every workplace, I have endured and witnessed a culture of marginalizing black and global majority workers, without repercussions. Constantly having to compromise and moderate our behaviour, constantly having to accept that any complaints of racism will not be taken seriously, constantly having to accept younger, whiter colleagues taking more hours but with less experience; all without the protection and due process afforded my less-melanated peers.

My experiences as a parent and teacher, and my children's experiences as athletes within UK sports, highlight a clear problem at every level. The fact that we have so many successful black athletes is not a credit to these institutions, it is despite them. Too many 'old- boy', nepotistic, outdated networks exist purely to maintain the mediocre status quo.

You ask why there are so few black swimmers?

The whole system needs an overhaul if you want a fair and true representation of the talent this country has to offer.

Jacqueline Antoine.
Swimming and aerobics instructor, personal trainer, and mother.

Jacqueline is a natural competitor and athlete who has been a swimming teacher for twenty years. Throughout her varied career she has coached many sports, including triathlon. Her hopes for the future are to build a private swimming pool so she can share her passion for swimming with her community.

OUTDATED NETWORKS EXIST PURELY TO MAINTAIN THE MEDIOCRE STATUS QUO

Elis Jones

HIGH-SCHOOL PUPIL

A Lesson in Racism

I go to a Welsh-language school in Cardiff and it isn't very diverse.

Before I was 13, this had never bothered me. I'd always felt different from the people around me, but I'd never thought anyone hated me because of it.

One day, I was making my way back from lunch to my class when a group of about ten boys in the year above started following me. I could hear them whispering and pointing at me. I decided to ignore them and hoped it wouldn't happen again.

The next day, as I got on the school bus, they all burst out laughing and pointed at me. I was embarrassed and thought I might have something on my face, but I didn't. I was also really confused – I'd never even spoken to them so I didn't know why they were targeting me.

At lunch on the same day they followed me again, but this time they started making noises and shouting out names of any black male celebrities they could think of: Idris Elba, 50 Cent, Ashley Cole. I couldn't understand what they were talking about at first. Then I realized: to them, all black people look the same.

They carried on for the next few days, naming more and more celebrities of colour – they didn't even have to be black; some were Asian!

Eventually, I told my mother about it and she was furious. She begged me to let her phone the school, but I wanted to handle it myself. She agreed, but said if it wasn't stopped immediately she would have no choice but to deal with it.

The next day, they started shouting names again and I asked them to stop. They just stared at me, then one of them ran up and ruffled my hair. His friends started laughing, then they all ran away.

That night I decided I wasn't going to put up with it any more and discussed it with my mother. We decided what I would do when it happened again.

So, when they started, I looked the ringleader in the eye and said, 'Why are you doing this to me? Oh, hang on, of course – it's because you're a racist!' He looked really shocked and denied it. I then walked straight to the headmaster's office and told him what had been happening.

He immediately went to their class and asked them why they thought it acceptable to victimize anyone for the colour of their skin. He warned them that racists weren't welcome in the school and if it ever happened again, they would be asked to leave, permanently.

That day, one of them came up to me and asked why I'd accused them of racism. I said, 'Why do you think?' He walked away without saying anything else.

After that they didn't come near me and luckily, it hasn't happened again.

Elis Jones.
High-school pupil.

Elis is passionate about acting and his overriding ambition is to be a successful actor.

Dr Lorna Cork

EDUCATOR

I Do Not, Thank You

I do not wish to share my experience of racism, thank you. I have no desire to recall the first day in a glistening education senior leadership role, when I swiftly recognized that although I had been offered the job, there was no intention to offer professional recognition, support, or even basic resources. My 'office' was devoid of a desk, chair, or telephone on my first day. I was informed that this was a logistical 'error'. Let me not identify any specific organization. Nor do I intend to delve into depths of despair or be deemed guilty of what education policy terms 'victim narrative' (Department for Education, 2020).

My focus is on conveying how unwelcoming, ice-cold, organizational cultures and individuals have been rendered less hostile, and harmful intentions diminished by the respect, warmth, and achievement of students. It is this that has kept me buoyant in education for over thirty-five years.

'Role model' would not necessarily be the first term in students' minds, or mine,

as an English teacher, Head of English, or member of the Senior Leadership team in London. I was simply bringing my authentic, Jamaican-born, black-British self to the roles; as I did decades later in the West Midlands as Senior School Improvement Adviser; and later again, working with the university sector. Some university students used 'role model' to depict me and nominated me for a 'Superstar' award.

To Mr Pseud, I was not a superstar. I remember the barely audible disparaging remarks under his breath about the predominantly black, working-class area where he knew I and many of our students lived. Let me relay the *friendly* advice to 'Remember, you're a senior manager now', on seeing me in animated discussion with students over lunch. Even at that early stage of my leadership journey I was aware that not all advice should be heeded. Had not a manager in a previous job asked, 'Why are you in such a hurry?' when I sought endorsement to attend a leadership preparation programme? Happy for me to continue leading whole-school initiatives without financial recompense, she was not willing to support my professional development.

As a somewhat ironic twist, we both turned up to be interviewed for a leadership position, years later. Not wanting to show off, who do you think got the job? Yes, it was me.

I would love to have heard her thoughts on learning that I had secured a place for a Doctorate in Education PhD at the oh-so-white, oh-so-middle-class, oh-so-prestigious University of Cambridge. Now, there is a tale I will not be sharing here. Perhaps a snippet:

1. It was at Cambridge that I learnt to like champagne; and

2. I was elected Vice-Chair of the African Caribbean Society and pioneered a community engagement project through which our graduates mentored local students.

Imagine if a black woman, not wealthy but prepared to take a risk, had not acted as guarantor in the event I did not obtain the funding for which I had spent months drafting a proposal. She and you are, no doubt, pleased that I was indeed awarded the ESRC Scholarship. In a phrase from my Jamaican, hugely supportive mother and our staunchly Roman Catholic upbringing, 'The Lord is good!' It was fortuitous, or God's grace, that my dissertation supervisor was Professor Donald McIntyre. Deceased now, Scottish, white- British, (never inadvertently call him *English*), he was a model of intellect and instinctively inclusive.

I was often the only black person in my jobs, especially leadership roles. There was always one or so of the predominantly white workforce countering, instead of colluding in the intersectional '-isms' that were hurled in my direction. They tended to be unobtrusive, supporting behind the scenes, while I blithely strove to implement more inclusive systems and practice, and continued to advocate on students' behalf.

Many who share my black-British background will not need me to elaborate on my experience of racism. We are no longer surprised at the similarity of experience, irrespective of sector.

Researchers and policymakers across decades evidence patterns of black exclusion, inequality, and 'miseducation', conceptualized as underachievement. You really do not need me to remind you of the reams of research enquiries, books, academic papers, reports, and rarely implemented recommendations.

Let me pause. Let me offer a toast (be it champagne, rum punch, or non-alcoholic sorrel) to students, to the younger generation; to me; to our older influencers; to those whose lives were needlessly shortened; and to those physically with us, still 'achieving', advocating, striving, leading, educating, and learning.

Dr Lorna Cork MBE.
Educator.

Dr Cork has over twenty-five years of success as an educator, and is highly sought after as an education and leadership consultant.

Dr Robert Beckford

ACADEMIC, THEOLOGIAN, AUTHOR AND FILM-MAKER

Dad

'I will put you on a banana boat back to Jamaica!' retorted Mr Brady, my design technology (DT) teacher. This statement came from a classroom experience in 1976, my first year in secondary school, and my initial encounter with the discipline of design technology. I was struggling to prepare the design for a metal candleholder, made from an aluminium square and screw to hold the candle aloft – this task is the introduction to DT for most children. I could not make precise the 45-degree angles for each corner of the squared paper we were using for practice. When I asked the teacher for help, Mr Brady's response was emphatic: 'If you don't get that design right, I will put you on a banana boat back to Jamaica!'

From the location of the limited educational scholarship of the period, Brady's behaviour is one of the numerous components within a racist educational system which, among other things, contributed to the subnormalizing vast sways of African-Caribbean pupils. The kids in my class had a mixed response. Some of the thirty 11-year-old children congregated around the workbenches laughed; others,

particularly the black and brown children, embarrassed and afraid, fixed their gaze on their designs and said nothing. The story does not end here.

At home in the afternoon, I recalled the encounter with Mr Brady to my parents. My parents' response to this incident differed, but was nonetheless complementary. My mother determined to double-up on her protective prayers for my siblings and me in the school. As a devout black Christian woman and founder of several churches in her denomination, prayer was a tactical weapon, which German theologian Dorothee Sölle would later describe as the 'protest tradition of prayer'. In contrast, my father's response was a different type of active outworking of his understanding of his faith. With the calm of the Yoruba spirituality that gave birth to the practice of the 'cool' that Joel Dinerstein talks about, he informed me that he would like to 'talk' to Mr Brady the next time I was in his class.

My father signified that when he said the word 'talk', it did not mean having a conversation with someone. Instead, it was a statement of intent to address the issue in a way that would resolve the problem once and for all. Semantic complexity is a feature of the Jamaican language.

My father was not intimidated by the school system or schoolteachers. He did not entertain the working-class deference of his peers, and as a trade unionist had strong views on hierarchy, power, and the problems of the Jamaican diaspora within the British working class. He was a builder, a scaffolder by trade, whose natural muscularity and athleticism was enhanced by years of long physical labour, nourished by 'hard' Jamaican food. He did not overpower those in his presence with his physicality. Still, as a Jamaican 'Westmorland man', he could string together a selection of critical words, phrases with a level of intensity and malice to frighten the devil.

True to his word, during the next design technology class, my father knocked on the classroom door and asked if he could have a 'word' with Mr Brady. There were no security gates at schools in the late 1970s, and it was not irregular for parents of children to seek out their children for medical appointments or other legitimate reasons for leaving school during the teaching day. The design technology block was at the front of the school, and access to it unencumbered.

Mr Brady returned a few minutes later. His face was red from blushing and his demeanour shaken. I discovered later from talking to my father that he had asked Mr

Brady if what I had recalled to my father was right, and if that was the case, would Mr Brady like to put my father on the boat, right now? Mr Brady fell silent and returned to the class.

As the Jamaicans say, my father's 'back-a-tive' (having our backs) was a severe deterrent to Mr Brady. Neither my black nor brown classmates, nor I, received any negative racialized comment from Mr Brady again.

References
Coard, Bernard, *How the West Indian Child is made Educationally Sub-normal in the British School System*, New Beacon Books, 1971.

Dinerstein, Joel, *The Origins of Cool in Postwar America*, University of Chicago Press, 2017.

Lalla, Barbara, and Jean D'Costa, *Language in Exile: Three Hundred Years of Jamaican Creole*, University of Alabama Press, 2009.

Watson, Tim, *Caribbean Culture and British Fiction in the Atlantic World, 1780–1870*, Cambridge University Press, 2008.

Dr Robert Beckford.
Academic, theologian, author and film-maker.

Prof. Beckford is a BAFTA award-winning documentary film-maker and a founding member of *Black Theology: An International Journal*. His research explores Pentecostalism, Rastafari and black music culture, examining the intersection(s) of religious experience, cultural expression, and political action.

Carmen Smart

FORMER INTERNATIONAL SPRINTER

Following the brutal killing of George Floyd, in May 2020, I was unable to shake off a feeling of melancholy that consumed me. We were in the midst of a countrywide lockdown due to the coronavirus pandemic, and I found myself sitting in my garden on a beautiful spring day lacking motivation to undertake any tasks. I remember thinking that if Martin Luther King had stepped back onto earth today, he would have thought he had only been asleep for a short time, as nothing much had changed in over fifty years. I certainly didn't think that as I was approaching my sixtieth birthday, we would still be facing violence and hostility just because of the colour of our skin, as we had when I was growing up in the 1960s and 1970s.

My father was one of the first draft of West Indians to come to this country, before the Windrush Scheme, when he answered a call from the British Government in 1944 for conscription into the RAF and, at the age of 19, he left his mother in his native Jamaica and travelled to the UK. He was stationed at RAF St Athan, in South Wales, and

when he left the RAF, he moved to Barry, where he raised his family. Growing up in a small town in Wales in the 1960s was challenging due to the ignorance of small-minded people, who believed that it was okay for them to spit at us, call us derogatory names, and throw stones at us just because our skin was a different colour. I don't think I knew what racism was when this sort of stuff was happening to us on a daily basis, but I realized it was insulting and decided to fight back – literally. Every time kids called me names, I would run after them and grab hold of them, ask them to repeat what they had said, and make them apologize. I'm horrified now that I reacted in that way, but at the time it left me feeling satisfied that they wouldn't do it again.

The earliest indirect racism I can remember was in the local church we used to attend. My parents insisted that we went to church every week, when the church service included Sunday School for children. Once a year they had prizegiving day when prizes would be awarded for best attendance in different age groups. Despite the fact that we

attended Sunday School every week, neither I nor my brothers or sisters ever won a prize. It didn't make sense to us at the time and, as children, we couldn't understand why we never won, but later on in life it was obvious that we were never considered worthy of being awarded a prize.

I was always interested in sport from a young age and displayed a talent for sprinting. I joined the local athletics club and dreamt of competing in the Olympic Games and winning a gold medal. Unfortunately, I didn't achieve my Olympic dream, but I had a successful career in athletics with no memories of racism. At the age of 16 I needed to choose a career path, but I really had no idea what sort of work I wanted to do. I didn't really want to work in an office and with my love of sport I decided I would like to be a physiotherapist, as I was interested in rehabilitation and recovery from injuries. I had a meeting with the careers officer in school to discuss my options and when she asked me why I wanted to be a physiotherapist, I nervously replied: because I liked meeting people. Her next words have stayed with me from the age of 16 until now, when she said, 'You can meet people working in Woolworths.' This response was like a punch in the face and I left the meeting believing that I was only good enough to work in a shop, whereas my white friends came out of their meetings with career

plans and excitement about their futures. My father always used the term 'colour bar' and I never understood what it meant at the time, but I later realized that it was a system I lived through.

There have been small improvements, which were confirmed when my daughter told me she doesn't feel like she's suffered racism, but there is still a long way to go in the fight to prove that black lives matter.

Carmen Smart.
Former international sprinter.
Carmen competed in three Commonwealth Games for Wales. Her athletic highlight was winning the bronze medal at the Commonwealth Games in 1986, as part of the 4 × 100-metre relay. She also held the Welsh 100-metre record in 1989.

Dr Vanessa Apea

CONSULTANT PHYSICIAN

Ready to Rise

Watching the mini-series *Roots* was a rite of passage in my family. My late grandfather insisted we watch it together, believing every black person should watch it, learn from it, and never forget it. I clearly remember the horror I felt witnessing the sheer brutality and injustice of slavery as the episodes unfolded. The images of Kunta Kinte and his descendants being dehumanized continually are forever etched in my memory.

Since then, seeing the injustices that black people have experienced when simply trying to live their lives has been painful, and has stirred cycles of anger, disappointment, and frustration. Yet, after these moments of despair, I would move on. George Floyd's murder,

however, made me truly stop. It evoked such a visceral and unparalleled response that took me many weeks, if not months, to unpack and process. A word that kept going through my mind was 'embodiment,' a concept described by the sociologist, Professor Nancy Kreiger. I had heard her referring to this in a lecture as the way we literally embody *biologically* our lived experiences, thereby creating patterns of disease. Black communities were collectively and visibly 'embodying' the trauma of this murder and I couldn't stop wondering how long it would take us to truly recover.

Like so many, I have asked myself why this event, and not another? Was it because it collided with me seeing first-hand, as a medic, the disproportionate impact of Covid-19 on black, Asian and other racially minoritized populations, together with what I felt was little action to respond to this clear health disparity? I'm still not sure.

What I do know is that I stopped. And then, a well-hidden and sealed Pandora's box opened and packaged memories of discrimination came oozing out. I realized painfully that there had been many examples in which I had been accepting the unacceptable: I had been glossing over the daily micro-aggressions I experienced. I would roll my eyes internally and suppress any anger or frustration and move past it. I had believed this acceptance was part of my innate resilience, recognizing that it stemmed from the micro-aggressor's ignorance and bigotry, and knowing that I was not the problem.

I've never really had difficulty talking about race, calling out white privilege where I saw it, and have always felt proud to be black- British, telling anyone in my presence for more than five minutes that I had Ghanaian blood running richly through me. But I suddenly felt that my tolerance level had been set too high, and that maybe I hadn't called it out enough.

Compounding this sadness was the harsh diversity of the responses to George Floyd's murder. How could everyone not agree it was wrong? All this fuelled my belief that to so many of the world, black people are still seen as inferior and we are simply not valued. I couldn't shake the feeling that no matter how far I advanced in my professional career, to many I would still not be regarded as an equal. My being black overrode everything. As the reflections of the Black Lives Matter movement continued and the conversations of diversity and inclusion expanded, rather than feeling seen, I increasingly felt 'lost in BAME', where my voice, opinion, and lived experience as a black woman in the UK were minimized. This is because I think that there is a definite hierarchy amongst racially minoritized groups, with commentaries and politicians repeatedly using the term 'BAME' to exclude, rather than include, the black voice. When trying to describe my thoughts to a colleague I said, 'I want people to see me, see all of me, but not define or limit me because of the colour of my skin.'

Then, one day, something just happened. I can't pinpoint the date or even the month, but there came a deep shift in me, channelling the words of Maya Angelou: 'Out of the huts of history's shame . . . from a past that's rooted in pain, I rise'. Specifically, from the anger, frustration, and sadness sprang hope. I was, and, still am, filled with an overwhelming determination to contribute to the change I want to see. Michelle Obama said, 'Do we settle for the world as it is, or do we work for the world as it should be?' I choose to work for the world I want. I will do my part in my space. I want the voice of our communities to be amplified. I want a better world for my kids, for my wider family, friends, and for me. I will not settle. We must not settle.

Dr Vanessa Apea.
Consultant physician.
Vanessa is the clinical lead for Sexual Health at Barts Health NHS Trust, and is also an honorary senior lecturer at Queen Mary University, London. She is on the medical board for NAZProject, a charity that aims to deliver culturally specific sexual- health services for minorities.

Revd Jide Macaulay

I am a black African, British Nigerian, openly gay man, HIV-positive, queer Christian theologian, and an Anglican priest in the Church of England.

I had waited seven years following my ordination to be able to add 'I am a priest'. And the journey of obscurity was not enough. I have had to fight for many things, perhaps from my mother's womb. Racism had a lot to do with the way I was treated by folks in the church and also by the hierarchy. My sexuality as a gay was also part of that, but when you think about the journey as black gay man, it is clear that race, HIV, and sexual discrimination can be problematic.

I have also endured HIV stigma by and from people of faith, many whom I call friends, who should have known better or at least put forward the teaching of Christ and made it central to their lives – love your neighbour as yourself.

Discrimination seems to follow me everywhere: I was born in London, but raised in Lagos from as young as 3 years old. My parents were students in the UK in the 1960s, when my older brother (now deceased), I and my younger brother were born.

Racism had haunted my parents to the extent that they decided to return to Nigeria, but with three British-born kids. I did not return to the UK until a few months before my eighteenth birthday. As I found myself settling down in south London – Battersea to be precise – I recalled that I had a very strong Nigerian accent and a beautiful dark skin that glowed in the sunshine. I arrived in the summer, so I loved the heat and rays of the sunshine. Within days of my arrival I had got a job cleaning at a medical centre in Chelsea. I didn't mind, but the stereotype was that I was better off starting my work career cleaning.

It wasn't long before I started to meet more white folks and in one of those moments, when I spoke about my roots, I was reminded that I am a 'black man'. In my confusion I had never recognized that as a fact, because in Nigeria being black was never mentioned, unlike tribes, or cultures, or tradition, or religion. People would know you if you were Yoruba, or a Christian, and perhaps which denomination you belonged to. But never was the colour of my skin a subject of much confusion.

About a year later, I had decided that I wanted to join acting school. I lined up a few interviews, including an interview at Glasgow University, and took an overnight sleeper train to the city, to be ready in the morning for the experience which included an audition. Like many people, I decided on *Othello* for my Shakespeare rendition; an act among other presentations. In the first round of auditions I didn't make the cut, but what surprised and shocked me were the comments of the judges: I was told that I had a speech impediment, but my accent was foreign and so was Othello. I pondered over that experience and the irony of a Glaswegian telling me I

had speech impediment. At the time I didn't know how to press charges or make noises about discrimination and racism. On my return to London I shared this with one of my tutors, who was white, and their response was that I should watch and listen to the ITV *News at Ten*, which at the time was presented by Trevor McDonald and Moira Stuart, who are both black. Years later, it dawned on me how racist my teacher was.

In light of George Floyd and the level of racism in America, as a black man in England there are no differences: racism is like my shadow because too often I am judged first by the colour of my skin with great disregard for my accent. In recent time, even in my role as a member of the clergy in the Church of God, white people have walked up to me with ridiculous compliments such as 'We can hear you clearly today', and some will offer suggestions on how to pronounce words so that I am clearer. I believe that many racist views come with a great misunderstanding of the diversity of humanity.

I now understand that I will always be different and unique in many ways, and the distractions about my race, sexuality, and HIV status are truly unnecessary.

The Revd Jide Macaulay.

Revd Macaulay is the founding pastor and CEO of House of Rainbow CIC. A Law, Theology, and Pastoral Theology graduate, he is an activist for HIV and social-justice causes, and the winner of the Black LGBT Community 'Man of the Year' Award.

Nigel Walker

SPORT EXECUTIVE

A School Day in the 1970s

I went to Rumney High School, attending between 1974 and 1981. It was a large comprehensive school of 1,400 pupils back then, with just a handful of black families in the immediate catchment area. It is fair to say that not a week went by without me being racially abused in some way, shape, or form. Some of it took the shape of *soft* name-calling and teasing, which after a while I was simply able to shrug off as normal; then there was the more aggressive and 'in-your-face' abuse, which told me that 'my sort' were not wanted here and that we should go back to where we came from!

There is, however, one day which is seared into my memory and that occurred in 1977, when I was taking my normal route through the school to attend lessons, when I was confronted by the words 'N*****S OUT' painted in three-foot-high letters on the outside of the gym wall. It was perfectly placed to gain the maximum number of sightings, since the gym was located on the main thoroughfare as pupils walked from one side of the school to the other. It took two or three days for the school to arrange for it to be painted over, and even then, it was possible

to see what had been written underneath. I lost count of the number of kids who asked me how I felt about it: some of my closest friends genuinely caring about how I felt, whereas a number of the others thought it was funny and were looking for a reaction.

It was not mentioned during assembly in any of the days following the words first appearing, and not one teacher or member of staff enquired how I felt, or condemned the actions of the perpetrator. I think the school staff just did not know how to respond so they did nothing. That is mirrored today when the BLM movement provokes the response that 'all lives matter'. There is an education and level-of-understanding gap, which needs to be addressed before we, as a nation, have any chance of bringing about a more equal society, where opportunity and potential are not based on your skin colour, where you grew up, or the school you attended.

There was one good thing to come out of the incident, and it's probably the biggest contributor to the drive and determination that I have today – it taught me that I could not rely on the authorities to ensure I would have a fair shake in this world, and that I

CONCERTED

EFFORT

needed to work harder and be more focused than the person next to me if I was to make the most of my potential.

As I say, the nation my children have grown up in has made progress, but surely the time is right for us to make a concerted effort to address the inequalities that still exist, to ensure that future generations are on a level playing field.

Nigel Walker.

Sport executive.

Nigel found fame in two sporting disciplines: as a sprint hurdler, he represented Wales at the 1984 Summer Olympics; and as a rugby union player, he won seventeen caps for his country. He is currently National Director at the English Institute of Sport (EIS).

Teleica Kirkland

CREATIVE DIRECTOR AND LECTURER

To Just Be

Navigating the world when black comes with a particular set of challenges and rules, some spoken, most unspoken, but all of them fully understood. The conclusive perception is that black skin is a problem to someone somewhere, and so it's best to stay where you are put, to minimize the dissent your skin will naturally cause. Arriving en masse to the UK in the 1940s, 1950s, and 1960s prompted several organizations to suggest ways in which we could reduce ourselves, so as not to upset the natives. This ideology of reductionism and self-minimization was promoted as a way for black people to demonstrate their decency. But in effect it enabled us to further absorb the racist belief that we were frightening and so needed to be contained.

Acknowledgement of racism in the UK is like the greatest exercise in communal gaslighting there ever was. Mainstream culture and various comments on every news article and social- media post will swear blind that racism doesn't exist, while accusing those who feel it instinctively of 'playing the race card'. It's exhausting and it's hard to catch breath. Traversing this landscape is a constant exercise in questioning one's own sanity.

Racism's effect on me manifested itself in a myriad of ways. Most acutely through the realization of what I could do and where I could go. I am a single-parented, council-estate child, born of immigrant parents, who knew education was important, but didn't have the means or understanding to show me how to get it. Nevertheless, it was drilled into me that however it happened, I was to reach the highest pinnacle I could. However, my institutions of learning, and the opportunities afforded to me, were not so assured of my upward trajectory, and the rhetoric of reductionism continued to follow me throughout.

A little brown-skin, picky-head gyal from the estates is not supposed to do well at school, and so inevitably I didn't. White supremacy and classism formed a toxic mix that expected me to stay in the enclave I had been assigned. I was not to step out of line or get above myself, but my curiosity and inability to sit still got the better of me, and off in the pursuit of adventure and an artistic education I went. Yet, the further I went, the fewer black people I saw. I realized that I was becoming the token, the only black person in the room, in the building, in the institution! Racism, reductionism, and self-minimization had infected all of us.

Underrepresentation is so rife outside the places black people have been designated to occupy; our presence in places we do not usually frequent still elicits fear, sidewards glances, open stares, awkward smiles, and overly enthusiastic acknowledgements, in an attempt at forced camaraderie. Underrepresentation has those who are underrepresented not trusting or believing the validity of our worth when we do reach the pinnacles of success, or worse, reducing or denying our blackness in a belief that doing so will help us to fit in. More reductionism.

It would be easy to say, don't shrink yourself, go wherever and be whoever; be big and bold, and loud and boasy, but that isn't always easy. Some of us have full confidence and sometimes the support to reach greater heights, but often this reveals other industry-based challenges and expectations that come with being from our designated places. I feel the weight of this perception and all perceptions that my skin encourages, and I'm left wondering, is there a place in the world where I can just be? Can I be black, and creative, and happy, without having to be in defence of my skin or my culture, and without having to be a source of exploitation, curiosity, derision, or concern?

I long to throw off the mental shackles of perception and expectation, and open my chest, take a big inhalation of breath, and let the air of that inhalation carry me away to far-off lands, where I can live in full realization of myself. In the sun, smiling, laughing, dancing. Not being told I'm too loud, or too sexual. Not being expected to have the best rhythm or know the latest moves. Not being expected to be cool or respectable. To just be, where I am free, to choose whoever I want to be and do whatever I want to do, allowing my natural effervescence to find its rightful place in the ether.

Teleica Kirkland.
Creative director and lecturer.

Teleica is a fashion and textile professional, who has worked with Vivienne Westwood and for the Victoria and Albert Museum. She is the founder and Creative Director of the Costume Institute of the African Diaspora. Teleica lectures at London College of Fashion, and has travelled throughout Africa and the diaspora, making links with designers and practitioners.

Fiona
Compton

PHOTOGRAPHER,
ARTIST, FILM-MAKER
AND HISTORIAN

F

The Outside Children

They come from a place
    Where mothers leave their children behind to rebuild Queen's empires,
    Destroyed by wars of tyrants
    Where barrels replaced parents filling empty hearts of children's desires,
    From the lost hard-working migrants.
    When you held the hand of your estranged father,
    It felt rough and weathered from working the soil.

FROM THE LOST HARD-WORKING MIGRANTS

Across the seas he would wonder farther,
    Now in Massa's land he would bend and toil,
    Feet blistered on his search to find a bed,
    Through the grit and through the fog.
    The sign reads, 'No Blacks, no Irish, no dogs',
    There is no good place to lay his weary head,
    They come from a place that had less and less daddies and mothers
    To read you bedtime stories under the moon, >

Because they tended to children of others,
  'Don't worry, baby', Granny say, 'they will send for you soon'.
  They come from a place,
  where Mother call her outside chil'ren and say,
  'Come home.
  I go give you a job
  and a place to stay,
  I need your help, tings here kind of hard,
  War mash we up,
  Pack up your tings, time for you to left yard.
  I go sen' a boat for you, tell your babies hush,
  The Dream Catcher ship,
  Dem call it *Windrush*.'.
  Tell your granny goodbye
  you may never see her again,
  Take one more breath of that earth,
  And say adieu
  to your old school friend,
  Land in the motherland
  One crisp cold morning,
  Sky as black as your skin,
  though the day dawning,
  Late-night ward work,
  Dem shout, 'I don't want that black nurse!'
  whilst back in a yard,
  Granny beloved pulled away in a hearse,
  'Come,' Mother say,

'We need you to fight war,
Once you know when it done,
You nah welcome no more,
Come drive we bus,
Sing us calypso,
And just don't make no fuss,
Play cricket with us,
Give we some of your culture,
We love your music!'
Tweet the flying vultures.

'Come,' Mother say. 'Come stay for a while.
  Long as you know
  You is de outside child.'

Fiona Compton.
Photographer, artist, film-maker and historian.
  Fiona is a London-based Saint Lucian. Her work explores the various disparities in representation of the African-Caribbean diaspora within art and mainstream media. Her films have been screened across the globe, winning several awards, including Best Documentary. In 2017, she launched her multidisciplinary project *The Revolution of the Fairytale*, which celebrates lesser-known heroes from black history, under the nostalgic platform of well-known fairy tales.

SKY AS BLACK AS

YOUR

SKIN,

THOUGH THE
DAY DAWNING

Maureen Nassoro

RETIRED NURSE

I moved to Wales from Jamaica in 1963, and began my nursing training in 1964. Initially, I felt very welcome. On the day of my interview, there was a white girl who was also waiting to be interviewed. She gave me her address and we went on to become firm friends, and even shared a room together in the nurses' home. The people in Wales overall were very welcoming.

I guess my first experience of racism was when I went to stay with a friend I had made in the nurses' home. Her parents took us out to a pub in Merthyr. When we walked in, it went silent and everyone just stared at me: it was clear I was not welcome and I felt incredibly uncomfortable. I don't think that they had ever had a black person in the area and they weren't thrilled with the idea. Needless to say we didn't stay there for long.

One incident I remember vividly was years later as a qualified nurse, when I was asked by a patient, 'How do you know when your hands are dirty?' I replied, 'The same way you know when yours are dirty'.

I was frequently asked by patients what my surname was. When I said the name on my badge, which happens to be a Scottish surname, they would say, 'That's an English name. That's not your proper name.' One incident which really upset me was when I admitted a patient, who was very poorly. She said, 'I don't want that black nurse looking after me.' At that moment I thought, *I'm a nurse. You are unwell. I'm here to help you and all you can see is my colour.* It was so hurtful. Sadly, there were many patients over the years who felt the same way. Some would even hurl racist names at me.

When racism comes from people you consider friends, it hurts that little bit more. After being invited to a colleague's home, the next day at work, she said, 'My husband asked, what does the black one eat?' She honestly hadn't considered that this might have offended me or hurt me. One morning after a night shift, I was feeling dizzy, so I decided to check my blood sugar. One of my colleagues said, 'Go on, let me see what colour your blood is.' When I did, she then said, 'Oh, it's red.' I was in disbelief. Did she seriously think that my blood was a different colour?

I can recall booking a hotel in London in the mid-1970s, only to turn up and be told that there were no vacancies. We were then given the address of another hotel. When we got to the new hotel, the accommodation was less than desirable.

I was so upset and in floods of tears, I knew there were vacancies at the hotel we had booked and that we had been turned away because of the colour of our skin.

The death of George Floyd has affected me deeply. The trauma of seeing a man killed in such a way was heartbreaking, I found it very difficult to get the footage out of my mind. I have nephews, brothers, and a grandson who live in America – this could have been any one of them. Following George Floyd's death, among many others I expressed my sadness, fear, and anger on social media.

It was both shocking and deeply saddening to find out the views of some people, and so hurtful to see the silence of white people who are your closest friends. I fail to understand how any human could witness this man being killed and not react, when I know that, had it been a dog or a cat being killed in such a way, they would have been outraged, and rightly so. I had friends reposting racist articles and saying all lives mattered, and just completely missing the point; failing to see that a man lost his life because of the colour of his skin, as have countless others. The reaction of my friends has shaken me, I must say. I felt very, very sad.

I don't understand how we are still having these conversations, trying to justify our worth as people of colour, trying to convince people that we should be treated equally, trying to show that our actual lives matter! I worry for my sons and my grandsons. I fear for them and that isn't right. In 2020, that just isn't right.

Maureen Nassoro.
Retired nurse.

Maureen was born in Jamaica and spent her forty-seven years of professional life dedicated to the NHS in the UK.

Sonia Obasogie

RECENT GRADUATE

Her Story

There was a girl . . .

She was born in Nigeria, where she was surrounded by people who believed in an equal community. Surrounded by people who looked every bit like her, who shared similar experiences and culture. Raised by her grandma, aunties, and uncles, who strived to ensure she was educated and content. Her father was absent and her mother in Germany, securing a better life and opportunity for her.

One day, she was informed that she was going to be with her mother and Caucasian stepfather in Germany, where her journey and experience of racism and emotional abuse began at age 8.

She arrived in Germany, feeling so hopeful, so eager, and intrigued about this new world. Seeing people who looked less and less like her. People she had never seen before. Feeling almost afraid of this new place, yet she was ready to accept.

The beginning and experience of this new world was amazing, but gradually it became a burden.

Her own stepfather, when he was drunk, slowly began to express his negative views of her people, her culture, and her beliefs. He started by calling her a monkey, worthless, and unwanted. Insulting her melanin, telling her if Hitler was alive, he would ask him to kill her and her mother.

Her melanin made him sick and he hated it. Threatening her and her mother every time he picked up a bottle of Bitburger beer. She witnessed it all, but was unable to speak out.

Him pointing a gun at her mother, reminding her that she was different and because of this she must die. She was constantly fearing for her life and she lacked the ability to eat. To the point where she became thinner and thinner with each passing day, not even looking her age anymore.

But when he dropped that bottle and was sober, he was the most loving man ever.

She refused to believe a man so loving when sober could become so violent, racist, and hateful when he picked up his Bitburger beer.

She lived like this for years, to the point that this was her normality.

The toxicity of the environment became her haven.

Unable to confide in others, slowing losing herself and her identity at such a vulnerable age. She was afraid of her new community and nobody else looked like her, apart from her mother.

Fearing the white man, she once was eager and ready to accept.

Until enough was enough, and she and her mother left for England, to start afresh and find a better community that accepted difference and diversity. Her new home and safe haven.

I am that girl.

The pain and hurt is a part of me.

I remind myself every day that everything happens for a reason.

God has a plan for my life. I am loved, I am worth more than the hurt, burden. and stigma.

I walk a path of success, a journey of development, self-love, and progression.

Sonia Obasogie.
Recent graduate.

Sonia aspires to be a businesswoman/counsellor and has a major interest in psychology. She is interested in helping and supporting individuals who have been through mental trauma.

GOD HAS A PLAN FOR MY LIFE

Dr Owen Williams OBE

CHIEF EXECUTIVE

White lives really matter to me both personally and in my working life and have been a de-facto reality for me since my mum gave birth to my happy little soul in Bradford, West Yorkshire, over half a century ago.

Please, indulge me the inevitable trip down Memory Lane as I write, but I need to take you back to a few years after I was introduced to the world. I recall walking home from my local school to see a full-blown, black, Nazi swastika painted against our brown back door. Alongside this symbol were the elegantly crafted words, 'Niggers fuck off home'.

Later that evening my dad, who originally came from Aberdeen – the Jamaican one – silently removed this unsubtle message from our council house. Nothing was said about it, nor did he call the police. There was no attempt to fight back, although ironically my mum comes from Accompong, the fortified, seventeenth-century Maroon stronghold.

It wasn't until a few years later that I came to understand that for my dad and mum the swastika moment was an accepted norm, as was the pervasiveness of 'Chalkie White',

the fictional black man who was the butt of Jim Davidson's jokes.

I read recently that an ageing Jimmy D. had no regrets about the persona he'd created and there are still many admirers of the underlying narrative he wove. My personal adventures with Chalkie came as the only black kid playing football for Saxton Avenue against Brafferton Arbor – the setting for the film *Rita, Sue and Bob Too*, where it was the norm for me to be referred to as 'Chalkie' in a bizarre south-Bradford version of patois.

Importantly though, although most of the white lads either openly laughed or quietly sniggered at the Chalkie-associated references, I do remember one white guy, Tony Brown, 'Browny', bravely saying, 'Leave it out lads.' His response is important as it reaffirms one simple fact that, although being a racist is not exclusive to white people, a white person who is prepared to go against the overt or covert tide of racism, can make a difference – it certainly did for me.

Fast-forward a few decades to the 8 minutes and 46 seconds that ended George Floyd's life, and it remains the case that the choices of white people are a dominant component when it comes to race and racism.

The findings of my own doctoral research in 2020 showed that when it comes to board-level appointments of black or brown faces, whatever the sector, the majority of senior white gatekeepers still firmly hold the keys and padlocks to the boardrooms.

If we are to make sense of the impact COVID-19 has had on our most deprived communities, or the loss of George's life, then the mostly white senior gatekeepers really do need to decide whether they are willing to step up and make a change.

This means they will need to avoid the temptation to simply undertake 'conscience-cleansing' activities or to become 'deniers of systemic racism', or for that matter, trot out the good old 'bad apples' rhetoric when a racist act is committed.

Sometimes it does feel like we are inhabiting a world reminiscent of the classic *Blazing Saddles* skit in which, early on in the film, the old white lady says, 'Up yours, nigger', to Bart, the black sheriff. Then, after Bart saves the day, she visits him under the cover of darkness and gives him an apple pie, only to return a few minutes later to say, 'Of course, you'll have the good taste not to mention that I spoke to you.'

Nevertheless, I remain hopeful that there is an immoveable force at play, exemplified by the following words, but you may have to search Google or the Sky Sports archives to find out *visually* what I mean.

At about 21.39, on 5 October 2017, Harry Kane scored a late winner for England against Slovenia, at Wembley. On the TV footage, Jordan Henderson comes over to celebrate with Harry, and behind the two players you see the big smiles of England supporters. Thing is, *all* the supporters pictured have black and brown faces.

This is what I mean by the reality of the 'immovable force', but the question remains: Can it deal with the 'unstoppable object'? As a simple example of the latter, between Monday and Friday click on a *Sky Go* app and find the CNN HD news channel. Search for the daily *CNN Tonight with Don Lemon* show, which usually follows the *Anderson Cooper* and *Cuomo Prime Time* programmes.

Ask yourself what is missing when all these shows become visible on the app. If you spot it, this is the day-to-day essence of the 'unstoppable object' which, it would seem, will always require us to keep on saying that, 'Black lives matter too'.

'Keep your pride. You can't be another colour butterfly' ('Black Butterfly', Sounds of Blackness).

Dr Owen Williams OBE.
Chief executive.

Owen holds the post of Chief Executive at Calderdale and Huddersfield NHS Foundation Trust. He joined the trust in 2012, from Calderdale Council, where he was also Chief Executive. Prior to that he was Chief Executive at Rossendale Council in Lancashire, and a Director of Marketing at Bradford Council.

Beverley Randall

ENGLISH TEACHER

Even as we struggle to make black lives matter again and again, we live in a country which fears the power that we represent.

As children our mum always told us, 'Some people won't like you because of this [pointing to our skin], but others will love you because they know you.' She had given us the beginnings of a 'power armour' to help us withstand the battles to come.

I was 7 years old the first time I heard the 'N' word. A boy at school called me this and the minute I came home, I told my dad. Angrily, he told me to go back to school, hit the boy, and return home. I did as I was told, but by then, I was too scared to ask what the word meant. Although I couldn't put it into words, I began to recognize that there was a difference between me and that boy that hadn't occurred to me before then.

I think I was 18, working in a bank as a copy typist. I walked into an office as a racist joke was being told and I caught the tail end of it. As the others realized that I'd heard something, the guy telling the joke turned to me and said, 'I'm not talking about you, Bev.

I'm talking about the others.'

'Yeah, and when I'm not in the room, I am the others!' I said, but the burning sensation in my chest and the tingling in my fingers betrayed my real feelings. I thought we were friends. It took me years to realize that he thought he was paying me a compliment.

Most of the time my racist experiences would come in the form of tiny arrows, as someone would touch my hair uninvited; shrink back from me if I asserted myself; tell me, 'If you don't like it, go back to your own country,' even though I was born here; not be served in a bar even though I was the only black person there. These little arrows would sometimes slide past the armour and land around my heart, creating wounds.

While Mum gave us wise words, Dad made us fact-check. He would select articles in newspapers for us to read when we became teenagers. 'Read this . . . What it say? . . . What it mean?' He taught us to look underneath the words, to smell the lies behind the double-speak, particularly when the articles related to black people. I'm grateful for the lessons they taught us, because outside of home and family, we didn't exist in the world we were born into. As children, we didn't see ourselves on television or magazines. We were a black puddle in a white sea.

The first time we experienced being in a place where the majority of the people looked like us was the first time we went to Jamaica, where our parents were born. It took several days before it dawned on us that this was why it felt strange.

The second time was a trip to Ghana. Books that I had read about our history became reality. Visiting the slave castle of Elmina, and hearing about the cruel and heartless treatment of our ancestors, was overwhelming. I felt as if every hurt I'd experienced attached itself to this moment. Tears flowed down my face without sound. After the tour, I stood on the shoreline, looking at the same view the ancestors had seen as they began the torturous journey to new lands, and I thanked them. I thanked them for living through all that they had been about to experience so that I could come back and thank them.

This is the power that our mum wanted us to understand: we come from a people who overcame immense struggles in order that we could live. This legacy of surviving against the odds is power. To laugh and cry and carry on is power.

To know your history gives you something solid to hold onto. Knowledge is power – personal power – and that is freedom. The freedom to be you in the midst of whatever is around you.

I guess if you don't understand that, maybe it is worth fearing.

Beverley Randall.
English teacher.

Beverley was a prolific theatre and television producer in the 1990s, known for Channel 4's *291 Club*, BBC's *Chef*, and ITV's *Comin' Atcha*.

Colton Belgrave

THERAPIST AND CHANGE MANAGER

'It Doesn't Rub Off'

I would say that I have always been considered as somewhat weird, slightly odd, or a little aloof.

As a child I would often spend hours by myself, creating imaginary worlds. Places where I felt normal, where I could thrive and be accepted. To my family, I was the quiet one, the mummy's boy, always wrapped around his mother's leg. Peering at the world from behind the folds of her pleated skirts was the only way to greet people; a timid

hand gingerly exposing itself for just long enough to be recognized as 'hello'.

Until I started school, seeking solace in the warm embrace of my mother was my only defence. At school I learnt how to hide, even in a crowd. It was a skill that I discovered purely by accident, on a day and time not unlike today.

I was 6, brimming with excitement from the night before. It was the day of my first school trip and as I stood in the gaggle of my chattering peers, the anticipation of sampling the unknown created a strange sensation in my stomach that I felt sure was about to erupt. Eyes wide, full of joy as the doors finally opened, and the teacher barked in our direction.

'All right, children.' Thirty pairs of eyes stared silently. 'We are about to leave, so remember to be on your best behaviour. Find yourself a partner, line up by the wall outside, and hold hands.' Her clipped Scottish accent hung in the room, mingling with the flurry of activity, mindless chatter, and muffled laughs that followed her words.

As I looked around the room desperately seeking the eyes that would link with mine, slipping from face to face, stalling on those with whom I regularly played, I slowly wilted with each furtive look away that silently signalled rejection. I realized that I was invisible and that I was hidden right there in plain sight. And as I watched the tide of giggling partners, buoyed by the joy of pairing, edge eagerly towards the door, I found myself following mindlessly, confused. Reaching the corridor, I fixed myself to the wall at the back of the line just before the growing din was interrupted:

'Is there anyone who does not have a partner?' A swift reply from the girl directly in front seemed to focus eyes on me. The parting crowd left me firmly in view of the craning neck peering above the bobbing heads to discover me. Miss was holding her by forearm, not wanting to touch the uncertain hand whose fingers had the habit of being found embedded in her nose or her seemingly forever-itching backside. The only other person without a partner. 'You two, pair up.' The subtle thrust of the tiny arm forward made it clear that we were to pair and as the quiet snigger began to build in crescendo, our eyes widened with the realization.

The snigger became a guffaw as she pulled away shouting, 'Eeew, miss, I'm not holding his hand! It might rub off on me!' My eyes flitted from side to side, not focusing, blindly watching the open mouths quivering and belching their approval in the form of a single communal laugh. I laughed too, not with my eyes, which moistened in the dim

light, but through a twisted facsimile smile that signalled my collusion and hid the pain careening through my innocence. And as I watched Miss struggle to barely hide the laughter secreted behind her eyes, it was clear that the worst that they had to offer was still preferable to me at my best.

The realization of words can be like castration, creating searing pain that neuters natural emotions, sowing colonizing seeds of collusion that stifle self-expression, hiding it away for fear of its imminent destruction. Words can make you duplicitous.

In that instant I realized that I was, and always would be, invisible. Invisible when it is convenient, like when there's a promotion, or when it's convenient not to say words like, 'It's because I don't like you . . . or 'We are just not the same . . .' I do become visible when there is a problem or when your unjust knee needs a neck to find. 'Different' is a word: it does not denote status nor engender privilege, but rather the subtleties of individuality.

I am invisible because I am different. I always will be. So do not fear my difference, for your difference does not scare me. Our differences make us unique. After all, difference 'doesn't rub off'!

Colton Belgrave.
Therapist and change manager.

Heavily influenced by his personal interest in holistic therapies, personal growth, and creativity, Colton used the events of the last year to explore his beliefs in culture, family, and life roles.

Joyce
Akpogheneta

PSYCHOTHERAPIST
AND COUNSELLOR

I Forgot!

He said, standing in front of the class, 'Africa did not begin with 500 years of slavery.'

It was a simple statement, but it fell like a bomb.

I forgot.

I spent my teenage years in Nigeria.

I knew of the empires, kingdoms, cities, and literatures of Africa.

I knew about the surplus of gold, copper, iron, and diamonds.

I adored the colours of our cloth against the endless shades of black, brown, and golden skin.

I planted okra, corn, yam, pepper, cassava, tomatoes, and groundnuts.

I picked mangoes, oranges, lemons, bananas, avocados, berries, and lime.

I drank water from springs that could trace their source from the Delta to the Niger River.

I was a child, grandchild, cousin, niece, sister, daughter, friend, kin of people whose DNA traced itself to antiquity.

I forgot.

The history of slavery, colonization, and racism allowed me to forget.

The constant need to be on guard against others who might hurt me because of the shape of my lips, the size of my nose, the texture of my hair and the hue of my skin allowed me to forget.

Africa did not begin with 500 years of slavery.

I do not define myself by 500 years of slavery and the inhumanity that has accompanied it.

I do not define myself by the lines drawn on a map by Europeans at the 1884 Berlin Conference.

I do not define myself by how the Western world sees me or how I see it.

I am not BAME.

I am not a minority.

I am a child of Africa.

I forgot, then I remembered.

I remembered what I forgot.

Infinity.

Joyce Akpogheneta.

Psychotherapist and counsellor.

Joyce is known for her work with young people and specializes in substance misuse, self-harm, suicide, domestic violence, resilience, and recovery.

Angela Jackson

RETIRED NURSE

I came to the UK from Jamaica in 1957, as a 14½ year old. When I was 16, my dad took me to a sewing factory to get my first job. The woman we saw – I suppose she was the manager – said it was 'all right' with her, but she did not know how her workers would feel about me. I asked my dad what was that all about.

'Don't worry about it. You won't be staying'.

It wasn't long before I learnt that that was her way of preventing people like me from getting jobs there, and a way of concealing her own racism. We went back to the employment agency and we were given another card: cake-box-making factory. There, we were greeted by a lovely buxom and very blonde lady with a great smile.

'Can you start on Monday?'

I spent a year and a half there as the only black girl and was treated like everyone else.

Then, I left to start my nursing training. Enjoyable and fun times. I made great friends. Eleven of us still socialize two or three times a year and we are well into our seventies and eighties.

However, as a third-year student nurse on night duty, I heard screaming coming from the paediatric ward bathroom. When I got there, I found a 4-year-old child curled up in the bath and a very upset nurse with him. She explained that she was bathing him and when he saw the palms of her hands, which were considerably lighter than the outside of them, the child became convinced that she was leaving her 'black' on him.

We tried to explain why that wouldn't happen and he calmed down enough to allow me to finish washing him (as my complexion was much lighter than hers), but wouldn't get dressed until he had checked in the mirror that no 'black' was left on him.

How sad that a 4 year old would react that way. What did he learn at home? I wonder if he grew up to be a nice young man and have lots of black friends.

Coming home from a trip with my husband and two children, we stopped to get some petrol on the motorway. A vanload of teenagers spotted us and started to name-call and gesticulate. When we got back on the motorway, the provocation and aggression started. The van drove alongside us. Then it would drive in front of us. Then it would slow down. This continued for a while. I decided to take down the number plate. I made sure that they could see me writing it down. Driving off at speed, three of the four boys dropped their trousers and spread their bottoms, while gesturing to kiss you-know-what.

When nursing as a senior midwife on night duty, one of my black colleagues was very upset and crying and came to see me. She told me that the white student midwife had asked

her, how did she know when her children were dirty and needed a bath. I reassured my colleague that I would speak to the student. When I did, I asked her what had prompted her to ask that question. She answered by saying that she didn't mean it as an insult and that she was just 'curious'. Her answer angered me more. Was she saying that black people looked dirty? I asked her if she waited until she smelt and her clothes were dirty and smelly before she took a bath. I told her to keep her mouth shut and think before she spoke, only ask questions appropriate to her job, and change her attitude and manner. To this day, I'm still not sure I handled it well.

I feel lucky that I have not encountered much racism in my life. Is that because I live in Wales and I have had a very successful career?

Sadly, direct experience of racism came a few months before I retired as a senior nurse from the NHS, thirty-six years after I started. I was reassuring a very ill patient and holding his hand during a procedure. He suddenly looked up at me and pulled his hand away.

'Get your black dirty hands off me.'

Shocked, I called my white colleague to take over. As ill as he was, he still saw my colour as 'dirty'.

As he left the area, I simply said, 'Good luck.'

Angela Jackson.
Retired nurse.

Angela was born in Jamaica. She retired as a Senior Nursing Sister in the 1990s, having dedicated forty years to the NHS.

Kai Harper

EDUCATOR

As a child of African-Caribbean descent, who grew up in north London during the 1990s and early 2000s, I must say that I was blessed. I use the term 'blessed' comparatively, in relation to the generations before me and to some of the young 'black' children that were a part of my school cohort. I have to give thanks to my mother, who made black pride an integral part of my life. She taught me very early on that black is beautiful, black is bold, and that we have a long and rich history whose roots start in Africa and stretch far and wide across multiple continents. I feel fortunate that, as a child and adolescent, I never had to question my place in this world. Even as a 33-year-old 'black' male, I still believe that the world is mine if I want it to be. No door is closed to me and no ocean is too dangerous to navigate.

This is not to say that I haven't encountered racism. I most definitely have, both covertly and outright. When reflecting on such instances I understand the nature of them to be the tail end of racist attitudes stemming from colonialism and post-Civil Rights movements. For some, blind ignorance and for others, a chosen disposition.

I refer to blind ignorance as the 6-year-old white Welsh girl, who was playing on the swings, in Bridgend, South Wales, next to me and my older brother. She must have had a revelation as, after playing alongside us for at least twenty minutes, she suddenly asked me, 'Why are you brown?'

I replied almost instantly and quite defensively, 'Why are you white?'

She seemed stumped at the time and was unable to give an answer and we all continued to play.

The chosen disposition that I refer to dates back nine years. I had just finished university in Leeds and had made my way back home to London with a friend. We had stopped for petrol just outside Chiswick and as I made my way to the shop, I noticed a girl looking at me. Naturally I looked back and smiled only to be horrifically disrupted from any endorphins I felt at the time.

'Oi! What are you looking at? That's my daughter!'

A very angry, short, and stocky-in-stature, middle-aged white man stood by his car squared to face me. I think at the time I replied, 'What's your problem? She was smiling at me first. It's not like she's your girlfriend, is it?'

What came next was the post-colonialist attitudes I referred to earlier, 'Come on then, you black bastard. Do you wanna fight? Let's go round the corner, big man.'

Fortunately, I didn't get into any further altercation with the prideful, ignorant man that day, although it did make me think, and still does to date, how different the outcome may have been if that had happened between 1948 and 1970, when slogans such as 'Keep Britain White' adorned local buildings and public houses. I am blessed that the generations before me fought for a world where my generation of black people would not have to suffer the same, unforgivable outcome as Emmett Louis Till.

Instead of looking back at my handful of experiences with disdain, I find that both joy and pride wash over me as I reflect on what it means to be black. My mind fills with the sounds of reggae music, Motown, and loud laughter. My nose and taste buds remember all the family events and parties adorned with delicious food. My fingers remember trying to be stealthy at sneaking meat out of the Dutch pot when Mum was in the other room. I smile as I look at a picture of young me wearing a Mark Morrison hairstyle.

As we near the end of 2020, I am proud of the inordinate amount of people worldwide who came together for the Black Lives Matter movement, to say enough is enough. Unfortunately, I fear that for some, it still isn't enough and I am saddened to know that we still have a lifetime of navigating and breaking down systematic racism in the workplace and in day-to-day life.

This is a challenge I approach daily with both optimism and frustration. I wonder where the world will be twenty years from now. I wonder when it will be safe to 'drive whilst black' in America.

Kai Harper.
Educator.

Kai specializes in special educational needs. He is the founder of Sen-space, an online platform to support families of children with special needs; a husband, and father of two. He recently completed his first novel, a young-adult fantasy adventure.

Yaw Amankona

STUDENT

I created this piece to reflect on emotion and the impacts people might feel from it. For example, as I'm trying to show in this piece, you could feel as if you're slowly being torn apart, or something like that, and I think this is how some people might feel when they've been affected by racism or discrimination.

Yaw Amankona.
Student.

Yaw is currently studying animation at university. He hopes to become an artist, cartoonist, or animator.

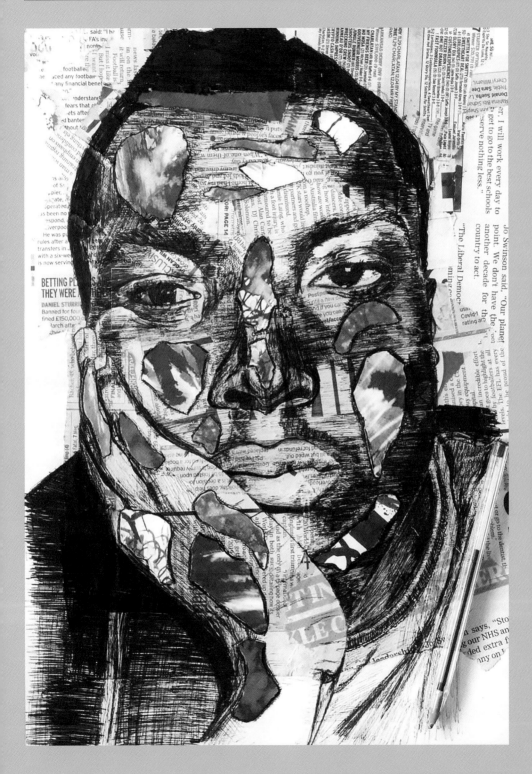

Pamela
Franklin

SOCIAL ACTIVIST

Shallow Breathing

I recall my days at school and how I longed to fit in 'with the crowd', but I had already been earmarked to be the new school's athletic captain, before even leaving my primary school!

I remember being one of only three black children who were selected into the first year at my secondary school. I became friends with the 'less desirable': they liked me because the others would not pick on them when I was around. It is only now, as I reflect, that I can see that the school was racially divided. I did not know what racism was – it wasn't a 'talk' that my parents ever gave me or my siblings.

In the council flats where I lived there was every culture. We children all went to the same primary schools, either Church of England or Catholic. Once we were back within the gates of our flats, all the children played together: kiss chase; two-balls; Irish

I HAD TO PROTECT MYSELF FROM THE PAIN

© *Aida Silvestri*

whip; soldiers; and more. At Christmas all the adults would ensure every child received a gift and we celebrated the festive season from our different balconies. Any adult was respectfully called 'aunty' or 'uncle', regardless of their race. I enjoyed my primary school and some parts of my secondary school, especially the athletic training and typing after school.

My secondary school did not focus on my academic ability, just on my athletic speed, which was why they selected me. The PE teacher Mr Green was strict on time-keeping and training, and treated everyone the same. As a girl I developed boobs at an incredibly young age, during a time when it was culturally considered the wrong time and age for a bra! Therefore, when I ran, I would place my arms over my boobs, take a deep breath, and not exhale or remove my arms until I got to the finish line. I remember Mr Green would shout, 'Breathe and move your arms!' I would just ignore him, thinking, *You don't know what it's like to run with boobs.* I had to protect myself from the pain. Nevertheless, it didn't stop me winning, although I would have been faster if my arms had been released and I had breathed.

The school merged when I was in the fourth year and that saw an increase in black pupils. I did make new friends, albeit in the athletic team, but most of the girls were older than me, which is why I joined the typing session between the end of school and athletics training and I sat quietly in the back repeatedly typing, 'The quick brown fox jumped over the lazy dog'. **>**

When I left school, none of the white friends that I'd protected kept in touch. I left school with two CSEs (Certificate of Secondary Education), a 45-words-per-minute typing speed on a manual typewriter, and the ability to run 100 metres in 12.8 seconds.

When at school I held my breath only to run, but on leaving school I had to hold my breath every time I went into the local Job Centre or recruitment agency, as I wanted to use my 45-wpm typing, but they wanted me to use my athletic speed and apply to be a 'tea trolley assistant' in the offices! Later, I removed a job-ad vacancy and went directly to the company, applied, and got a job as an office junior.

As the years went on, I faced discrimination in job opportunities, so decided to become a temporary worker. The start of the computer era opened doors as I had perfected my typing speed to 90 wpm, and this gave me the confidence to tackle any machine with a keyboard. I quickly learnt that anything with a keyboard was viewed as a 'female job'. I became known as 'the computer temp' and eventually applied for a job as a trainer for one of the agencies. I was an IT trainer only on paper, but not in person, despite knowing the systems better than the other trainers, and was tasked to be the technical writer, who wrote the training material. However, this allowed me to learn the systems inside out.

As a black person I soon learnt that I could never express what I didn't like: I had to hold my breath, as it could mean the difference between having a job or not, which I was told more than once. Eventually I became a trainer, was then head-hunted to be a training manager, and finally I started my own IT training business.

Fifteen years after leaving school, a candidate for one of my business contracts was the head teacher from my secondary school. I didn't know whether to call her 'Miss' or 'Mary'. Later I also hired the former head of the English department. Both of them had joined my secondary school the year after I had left.

As a black woman who is now older and disabled, I have faced challenges that have sometimes taken my breath away. Although I am no longer running, I must still protect myself from pain. I think the only time that I truly breathed was in the playground as a child, when I lived in the gated community and felt free.

Today I volunteer in a community group and I have learnt from my peers that shallow breathing is life.

Pamela Franklin.
Social activist.

Pamela is the founder of the Caribbean Social Forum, a non-profit organization which provides a space for social gatherings for the Caribbean community. Her organization was the Winner of the Community Organization Award in the Race, Religion, and Faith category of the National Diversity Awards 2017.

AS A BLACK PERSON
I SOON LEARNT
THAT I COULD

NEVER

EXPRESS

WHAT I
DIDN'T LIKE

Bishop Rose

BISHOP OF DOVER AND
THE BISHOP IN CANTERBURY

I watched that video clip. It was sent to me before the story broke here. And I was sitting there screaming, 'Get off him! Get off him!' I felt pain that a man – a man, not some wild animal – was lying there. He was already handcuffed, and yet his very breath was taken from him. He said, 'I can't breathe. Please, sir, I can't breathe.' But he wasn't heard. He wasn't heard because they didn't care. They didn't care because he was black, and they thought he didn't matter. And that's why we say 'Black lives matter', not because we are opposed to white lives, that's a nonsense. Let's all – black and white, pink and blue, old and young – stand together and say, 'People's lives matter.'

We want to live in a world where all lives matter – and all lives will not matter until we accept black people's right to be free. I don't want this just to be a protest and then we go back to our ordinary lives. We can't do that. We must stay discontented until we have structural change in all walks of life, in the economic structures, policing and criminal justice, education, health, housing, voting – all of it must change. We must call our politicians to account. Most of all, we must all live as though we mean it.

You can see from my garb that I'm a woman of faith. My faith is not just about kneeling in prayer. I pray all the time, but actually my faith teaches me that God created all humans, that God is interested in our lives, in justice and fairness. and whether we look after the most vulnerable in society.

People say, 'But look at that lot over there. They're fighting and knifing each other.' But if for years and years you are told that you are not valuable, then you will behave as if you are not. That's what we're seeing on our streets, played out in knife crime. If generations of young people are told by the way they are treated that they have no worth, they begin to believe it. We need to, as Bob Marley sang, 'Emancipate yourself!' >

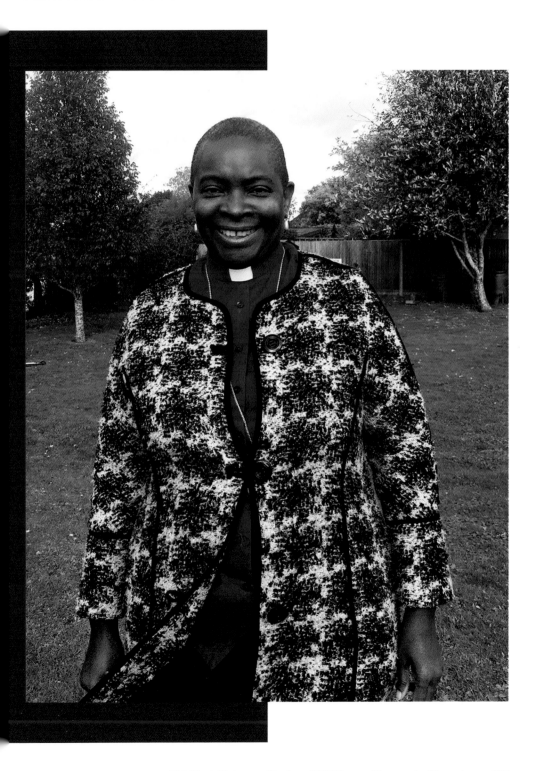

We've got to free our minds together and treat each other with respect. So, if you are ever in a gathering like this and you see someone taking things out to throw at the police or anyone else, talk them down, because it will distract from why you are there.

This country is amazing, but we are the ones who will make it great. The greatness will come by the way we treat one another. And right now, because we haven't been doing it right, it's not telling us about our greatness. So, I beg you to make sure we do it right. But I also say thank you for being out here, for owning the fact that our lives matter, for giving up your beautiful sunny day to say that George Floyd's life mattered, that the lives of all those who have died in a way they should not, mattered.

I wasn't always Bishop Rose Hudson-Wilkin. I, too, have had the pain of rejection. I too have been treated as if I have no worth. But I was damn lucky to have been born and brought up in Montego Bay, Jamaica. Because there I saw images of myself in all walks of life. I grew up knowing that I didn't have to just play sport, or music, but I could be anything I wanted to be. And that's what I want for our children – black and white, pink and blue, grey, or whatever shade they are. I want our children to grow up knowing that they can be whoever they want to be. We don't want

I SEE SOME OF YOUR PLAQUES:

RACISM IS

platitudes or nice words, we want action; the kind that enables and means that my grandchildren will have a different outlook.

I see some of your plaques: 'Racism is a pandemic'. It is a pandemic and we have been dying; dying in so many ways that are slowly killing the next generation. You can stop it. So, please, let's do that. And let's go peacefully. Let's not find somebody else to blame. When we go from here, let's go with a commitment that says, 'We are going to be the change that we want to see!' Don't push it onto somebody else. We are going to be the change. God bless you! Peace be with you!

Bishop Rose.
Bishop of Dover and the Bishop in Canterbury.

Born and raised in Jamaica, Revd Rose attended Montego Bay High School for Girls before later completing university in Birmingham, and then training for ordination at Queen's Theological College. She has served as a priest in Hackney and, in 2007, she was appointed as a Chaplain to Her Majesty the Queen.

A PANDEMIC.

IT IS A PANDEMIC AND WE HAVE BEEN DYING . . .

Michelle
Griffith-Robinson

FORMER INTERNATIONAL
ATHLETE AND OLYMPIAN

FIRE IN MY BELLY

TO ACHIEVE MORE

My mother left Jamaica at 21, with big dreams and hopes to become a teacher. Mummy did a U-turn and turned her loving caring nature to nursing. This was not an unfamiliar career choice for many educated black women of this era.

I could not have imagined leaving my parents and my siblings to come to another country where people chose not to embrace me because of my skin colour'!!

2020, however, is a year that has been unforgettable. We have seen life-changing experiences that have changed the world. I refuse to bend my head in dismay. Instead, I choose to stand tall, with my big piercing eyes, and my beautiful black skin, and maintain the 'fire in my belly' to achieve more.

I intend to role-model excellence, so that my mother's journey from the little fishing bay called 'Old Harbour' to the big city of London was not in vain!

The legacy will not end with *me*.

Michelle Griffith-Robinson.
Former international athlete and Olympian.

In Great Britain, only one other athlete has jumped further than Michelle in the triple jump. Now a lifestyle coach and personal trainer, Michelle is passionate about mentoring, with a mission to empower and rejuvenate lives.

Dr Judith Agwada -Akeru

CONSULTANT
ORTHOGERIATRICIAN,
PHYSICIAN
AND FASHION BLOGGER

I've really struggled to start writing about my experience of racism, as really, where does one start from?

But here we go.

I arrived in the UK fresh out of medical school, with a passion to save the world burning away in my heart, or some sort of odd feeling.

Decades before this time my father had been an intellectual, who was actively involved in anti-racist and pan-African activism in the United States. He would eventually move back to Africa to try to bring about a different kind of change; one where we would empower ourselves to survive better in a world where we are deemed inferior, thereby proving we're equal after all.

I was a product of this activism and on arrival was convinced I was immune to another man's perception of me, based on the colour of my skin. If this was social media, I would insert an emoji of a maniacal laugh here.

As a young house officer (first-year post-grad) I was like most junior doctors in that I had no clear career path in mind.

I was just happy to be starting my post-graduate training in a prestigious teaching hospital in the country.

My first day on the ward started like most would expect: I woke earlier than usual, wore my pre-selected outfit and set off for XYZ hospital. I had scored highly enough in the anonymized selection process to get my first choice of hospital, and in London too.

That morning I would have an encounter, which I would never forget.

We all lined up in our fresh XYZ white coats to be introduced to our consultants, including – and especially – a very renowned vascular surgeon.

As the rounds of introduction got to me, I had carefully prepared a small bio of my journey to XYZ, which I was waiting proudly and nervously to share. Sadly, instead of 'Doctor, can you tell us about yourself?' what I heard was, 'How did you get this job? I thought we had done enough to reduce the number of IMGs [international medical graduates] allowed into these posts'. What does one say to this? Another consultant quickly stepped in with, 'She clearly scored enough to get in'   >

This was the foundation of my foundation year; a year I spent facing various forms of racism.

One clear example of this was a day when the same lead surgeon requested an assistant in theatre and I volunteered to attend. On arrival, after scrubbing, he saw it was me and refused to have me assist him. His words exactly were, 'Tomorrow she will state on her CV that she assisted Professor XX in theatre.'

This pattern of behaviour would continue, with multiple episodes of comments such as,

I never shared this with anyone as I was simply ashamed that perhaps they were right and I was less, inferior, and just not good enough.

Time would pass and by my second year I was considering quitting medicine and just going back home.

A fellow international medical graduate contacted me to share how awfully she was being treated at her job. I couldn't believe that she was experiencing the same behaviour I had been experiencing. I confessed my story to her, and started checking how other black

'Maybe in your country this sort of activity can occur, but not in developed countries like here', for example, on giving gunshot and stab wounds as a differential for a vascular injury. You have to understand that these occurred regularly, and during clinical meetings, where I was the only black person in the room, there were questions, such as, 'When are you going back to your country? Don't your people need you more?'

I lost every iota of confidence; developed a terrible practice of second-guessing myself, and a stutter; and frankly became depressed. My only comfort were my two young children, who would look at me with so much love in their eyes; with them I was something.

doctors I knew were getting on. And believe it or not, they had mainly the same stories.

My friend and I decided it wasn't possible that we were all of inferior intelligence to our white peers.

We then elected to take the most difficult exam at that time just to prove that we were okay. I took mine and decided, after passing, that I would go all the way and become a specialist physician. Many colleagues from our community tried to discourage me, saying they would never let me through at the final exam point: a practical exam, a famous bottleneck for black physicians. But I just kept going and eventually, in February 2020, I qualified.

Don't get me wrong, I have faced racism constantly through my career. Being the only black person in the room at almost every training session, meeting, and so on, was daunting; and yes, I probably got more and more quiet, got used to sitting by myself and generally disappearing into the furnishings.

It has ranged from patients wanting a white doctor; to me being asked to not see a patient as they were not used to blacks, to avoid distressing them; to a junior doctor coming into our consultant office in the most recent week to introduce himself to his clinical

I delved into fashion mainly as a diversion and I somehow believed if an outfit was great, you would get an audience, irrespective of the wearer, and I started writing a blog. I also found the virtual world of fashion blogging impenetrable as a black blogger, so I sat back, thought about what I truly enjoyed about blogging, and decided I loved discovering new products and sharing about them.

I realized that artisans would sell you their products most often without caring about your race, as you would often only communicate virtually, so they would

supervisor – and walking right by me to the white colleague behind me, only to be told that I was the person he was looking for.

My solution to this problem was to challenge myself, to continue to empower others in my community by speaking of my experience, recognizing the new lone black person in the crowd and befriending them, and generally speaking up against racism as much as I can. Did I speak up as much as I needed to further in my career? No. I am not ashamed to admit that I am now in a privileged position career-wise and hence more able to speak up and challenge racism. I would like to see more people at the so-called table speaking up too.

have an impression of you before realizing who you are and that you are genuinely desperate to grow their business. On the same note, if you provide people with a good product or service, they will come to you.

I set up Maison Archives London based on this principle.

Dr Judith Agwada-Akeru.
Consultant orthogeriatrician, physician and fashion blogger.

Judith works for Barts Health NHS Trust. She has a specialist interest in age anaesthesia and silver trauma. Judith is the founder of Maisonarchives.com.

Tony
Hendrickson

EQUALITIES AND
SOCIAL JUSTICE WORKER

Déjà Vu

Human: consisting of people; the human race.

Humane: sympathetic; a warmly human understanding.

Humanity: all human beings collectively, the quality of being humane; kindness; benevolence.

During the summer of 2019, at my local corner shop. My young child (age 11) exited the store just before me. He stood just outside the entrance and as I finished my conversation, I followed him. I heard a shout from a passing car. It was an innocuous sound until I saw the look on my son's face. I immediately recognized that look; a combination of disbelief, hurt, anger. Still, I asked, 'What's the matter?' He told me that one of the passengers had looked at him and shouted an unambiguous racial epithet (my words) at him. Distracted, I had not heard the insult, but we both observed the three young females laughing as they drove off.

We slowly walked the short distance home during which time he tried to understand their motivation. 'I didn't do anything to them! Maybe they were drunk. They must be bullies. Maybe they are *just* racists.' Then came the emotion I understand all too well from my childhood: Why hadn't I heard it? Why was I talking to the cashier? His way of saying, why was I not there to protect him?

Déjà vu!

I reassured him that his anger, frustration hurt were legitimate, followed by my mantra, don't let them define you, do not let others characterize your humanity. This was not the first time my young son had experienced direct racial discrimination; it wasn't the last.

25 May 2020 Christian Cooper and Amy Cooper (no relation) in Central Park New York. The quarrel started because Ms Cooper did not have her dog on a leash, as stipulated for that specific area

leash, Amy Cooper threatened (African-American male) Mr Cooper, by verbally acknowledging the ramifications of her position against his. The talking point of this incident was the weaponizing of racial politics. When calling the police, Amy Cooper exhibited a cold, inhumane understanding of the dynamics at play.

Video footage of George Floyd's death due to the long, brutal, physical restraint conducted by the police went viral. The officers had clearly lost their humanity, could not see the human in their grasp, and therefore acted catastrophically inhumanely. Protests were swiftly organized by and with the Black Lives Matter campaign. The international allegiance with the BLM campaign was unprecedented. Of course, my child was aware of this murder, mainly via the news and discussions he overheard on the radio at home, and conversations in school. He is already only too aware of the racial dynamics underpinning this.

Déjà vu!

When I took my child to a socially distanced, peaceful BLM demo at the large centrally located park in our home city, I wanted him to see that many people care, have not taken leave of their humanity, and are willing to challenge inequality. On arriving we were almost immediately greeted by people and families that we knew. The crowd was visibly diverse and consisted of individuals, groups, and families listening and applauding the various speakers. As we left my son discussed the issues that had

stood out. He became increasingly angry and upset.

Inwardly, it distressed me to experience his palpable frustration, his fear, sense of loss. I encouraged him to speak as he saw things. I listened. Eventually he asked me questions. I responded as honestly as I could, telling my 12-year-old of incidents and experiences I had naively hoped I would not have to revisit in his presence. I told him about some of my experiences of racism; how at different times I had reacted and felt; when I had [often] felt unsupported and misunderstood; and the occasions I had been listened to, understood, even supported. The conversation flowed, but importantly by the time we returned home we were joking. I felt relieved and pained. I know life now is not exactly as it was when I was his age, so why do I feel a sense of déjà vu?

'The function of freedom is to free someone else' (Toni Morrison).

Déjà vu. Based on my own and familial experiences (and long before current incidents), I vowed to act for my own, my child(ren)'s and future generations' happiness. I cannot change the past; I can learn from it. I will strive for a better future.

Tony Hendrickson.
Equalities and social justice worker.

Tony's role is to advance projects, initiatives, programmes, and organizations that promote equity, access, and social justice for minoritized people and communities.

Who know better, do better.

JAMAICAN PROVERB

Part III
Making a Difference, Making Waves

Phyll Opoku-Gyimah

Arthur Torrington

Sharrion J. Francis

Lord Paul Boateng

M. Jay

Dotun Adebayo

Dawn Butler

Ali Abdi

Hermon and Heroda Berhane

Ron Shillingford

Trevor Phillips

Shaun Bailey

Pat Younge

Patrick Vernon

Nadine White

Vaughan Gething

David Lammy

Marcia Degia

Bonnie Greer

Phyll Opoku-Gyimah

EXECUTIVE DIRECTOR

I have always been reluctant to tell stories of how racism has impacted my life. Whether the individual instances of vitriol or dismissal, or the larger structural bludgeonings of the State, I've never really understood what the point is. Who do these stories serve? One might say that black people coming together to share how racism impacts them allows for greater understanding and connection, but this relies upon a performance of trauma and pain that white people have come to revel in. It's not enough that they are the arbiters of such horrors; they need to see us writhe, cry, and wince in public retellings of our pain. Perhaps speaking of instances of racism helps other black people understand they're not alone, though I've never felt particularly comforted by hearing these stories. Or maybe the telling of our stories is mounting evidence of the obvious, and might help build a case for some large-scale change (over 400 years' worth of evidence not being enough apparently). From whatever vantage point I examine it, I can't make the sharing of stories of racism make sense.

Which is not to say sharing our stories of racism is not helpful, just that I haven't yet understood the benefit. What bothers me about these requests for stories of racism, is they never come with an acknowledgement that these stories might be difficult to tell. There is an assumption, an inference, that our black experience is such that we are always ready to tell these stories, that reaching back into little compartmentalized boxes and bringing out blood-covered stories is as simple as opening one's mouth. There is a reason my experiences remain under lock and key, not least of which is the frequency with which they happen. If every racist remark taxi drivers, waiters, shop assistants, or colleagues ever made was just knocking around in my head for plucking and sharing, I wouldn't be able to move for the vertigo. And perhaps most crucially, asking black people to share our pain so often draws attention away from what thousands of instances have in common: white supremacy.

And I don't want it to be so normal to ask black people to share stories of racism. As Kevin Quashie argues in *The Sovereignty of Quiet*: 'As an identity, Blackness is always supposed to tell us something about race or racism, or violence and struggle and triumph, or poverty and hopefulness. The determination to see Blackness only through a social public lens, as if there were no inner life, is racist – it comes from the language of racial superiority and is a practice intended to dehumanize Black people.' >

THERE IS A REASON MY EXPERIENCES REMAIN UNDER LOCK AND KEY

I AM
STILL
BREATHING

So my question stands: who do these stories serve? Why are we not asked more frequently to share stories of tenderness, vulnerability, and love? Why are we not asked to speak to our dreams and our desires? What of our imaginations and our longing? What Quashie calls the 'voluptuous' interior life is cast aside, erased, and made unimportant when the value of black life – of black storytelling – is measured by our ability to perform pain. There is much more to my life than the racism that has so often blighted it.

The primacy of racist storytelling in the narrative of black life must not be allowed to stand, and must not be privileged over stories we actually want to tell about our lives. And if it's comfort we're looking for, if it's to know we're not alone, then there

are no better examples than the stories of solidarity, understanding, and love that abound among black people – those frequent moments in which an inherent, ancestral, visceral understanding gives way to a simple yet profound relief.

In fact, the moments of my greatest relief and release have always been in the arms of other black women, who have never needed me to recant for them the particularities of racism. We know all too well the contours, the shadows, and the pain of racism. Let it not be here, among each other, that we're asked to excavate these experiences – experiences that are allowed to be buried.

So, I have not given you stories of racism because I don't want to. I am still breathing because I am surrounded by people who shield me and who love me, because I give myself freely to those who will change the world, and because my life is not the sum total of what white people have done to me and mine. I am still breathing because I place a premium on my self-care, prioritize my wellbeing, and protect my peace. I am still breathing because I descend from a long line of warrior women, who refused to have their wings clipped, their dreams deferred, or their lives narrowly defined. I am still breathing because I am not done yet, and because I have a daughter to raise and a community to empower. Racism will not define my life; my legacy will.

Phyll Opoku-Gyimah.
Executive director.

'Lady Phyll' is the cofounder and director of UK Black Pride. Phyll is currently the Executive Director of the Kaleidoscope Trust, an international charity working to uphold and advance human rights for LGBT+ people, thus becoming the first black woman in the UK to lead a mainstream charity. Prior to this, Phyll worked for trade unions, focusing on equality. She is the editor of *Sista!* an anthology of writings by LGBT women of African-Caribbean descent.

RACISM
WILL NOT DEFINE
MY LIFE

Arthur
Torrington CBE

COMMUNITY ADVOCATE
AND HISTORIAN

THERE WERE NO RESTRICTIONS ON WHITE IMMIGRANTS

British Citizens unjustly treated as Immigrants in the UK

Even before members of the Windrush Generation landed at Tilbury Docks, Essex, on 22 June 1948, they were seen as 'coloured immigrants' by British MPs. The *Empire Windrush* became closely associated with 'coloured immigration', which was the term used by both Labour and Conservative Governments after the Second World War. 'Coloured' (black) people dominated MPs' discussions for the following seven decades and their decisions brought untold injustices to thousands of Caribbean settlers.

The Labour Government came to power soon after the war and intended to hinder attempts by Caribbean people to settle in Britain. There were no restrictions on 'white immigrants'. The *Empire Windrush* was one of many British troopships that brought people to the UK after the war. >

There were 110 mainly African-Caribbean ex-servicemen on the SS *Ormonde* that arrived in May 1947, and over 200 on the SS *Almanzora* in December 1947.

However, the *Empire Windrush* raised Whitehall alarm bells and there were more than 1,020 passengers on board the ship. The British Government took immediate action to dissuade others who were planning to settle in the mother country. A letter of 22 June 1948, sent by eleven Labour MPs to Prime Minister Clement Attlee, said:

An influx of coloured people domiciled here is likely to impair the harmony, strength and cohesion of our public and social life and to cause discord and unhappiness among all concerned . . .

'In our opinion such legislation or administrative action would be almost universally approved by our people.' (HO 213/244, J. Murray *et al.* to Prime Minister, 22 June 1948).

When the Conservative Government came to power in 1951, MPs increased the heat on 'coloured immigration'.

THE SCANDAL IS A RESULT OF MORE THAN SEVEN DECADES OF ANTI-COLOURED IMMIGRATION LAWS PASSED BY MPS

'This country may become an open reception centre for immigrants not selected in respect to health, education, training, character, customs and above all, whether assimilation is possible or not.'

'The British people fortunately enjoy a profound unity without uniformity in their way of life, and are blest with the absence of a colour racial problem.

The hard-working Caribbean men and women who settled in the UK before and after 1948 were often treated less favourably than 'aliens' because of 'racialism' (now called 'racism'). The British Nationality Act (July 1948) formally gave them 'citizen status' from

1 January 1949. They had left colonies that had been impoverished by the mother country for decades. Given that many of them had served King and Country in the war, the unwelcoming attitude tied in with the thinking of the day – 'No Irish, no coloureds, no dogs' – revealed the public's ingratitude and 'colour prejudice' (racism). In the 1950s, public discourse on immigration or immigrants painted a picture of 'foreigners', 'aliens', 'undesirables', 'inferior', and 'not one of us'.

Windrush passengers settled mainly in England and Wales in a similar way as the English did in Scotland, Ireland, and Wales. Welsh, Northern Irish, and Scottish settlers live in England and are British. The situation should not have been any different for Caribbean people who are also 'stakeholders' of the British Empire. Their ancestors helped to build it from the 1600s and the Windrush Generation contributed significantly to rebuilding Britain just after the Second World War.

The so-called 'Windrush Scandal' was inevitable because the Home Office disregarded the fact that every member of the Windrush Generation was British before and after 22 June 1948. They deserved the 'respect' accorded to Scottish, Welsh, Northern Irish, and Scottish settlers live in England and are British. To quote from *British Social Trends since 1900* (Halsey [ed.], 1993, p. 568): 'The legislation of the 1960s was rationalised and formalised into a new Immigration Act of 1971 . . . Those who had come before the Act came into force in 1973 were settlers and those who entered after were simply migrant workers. Immigration legislation had led to the establishment of discriminatory nationality laws.'

A proper understanding of colonial history and Britain's nationality laws from 1948 would have helped MPs and the general public to appreciate the fact that every member of the Windrush Generation settled here is a citizen. It was an act of gross injustice as thousands of them were made victims of the Government's 'hostile environment' and harassed by 'immigration enforcement/Home Office police', who readily saw them as 'suspects' because of the 'colour of their skin'. No Government compensation scheme can ever mitigate the loss and distress suffered, and less favourable treatment as 'illegal immigrants'.

The scandal is a result of more than seven decades of 'anti-coloured' immigration laws passed by MPs.

Arthur Torrington CBE.
Community advocate and historian.

Arthur is the director and cofounder of the London-based Windrush Foundation, a charity that, since 1996, has worked to highlight the contributions of African and Caribbean people, who were among the first wave of post-war settlers in Britain.

Sharrion J. Francis

CIVIL SERVANT

Darky from *The Messenger.* Golliwog. The other black people who worked here before were no good. They'll never let you on air with your hair like that; it's too ethnic. I don't like her either, but I have to work with her.

These are just some of the things I've had hurled at me since arriving in England from Jamaica aged 10. I was a shy outsider so it took me a while to realize that some people's reaction to me was due to my colour. But the clues were there. My primary school teacher never hid his surprise that I could actually read and write.

This low expectation continued into secondary school, where I was put into the lower stream with the other black, vaguely foreign, and working-class pupils. I was saved from mind-numbing boredom when I came top in most subjects and my mother insisted that I was moved up.

A similar battle ensued when I wasn't allowed to do O level English despite getting the same mark as a white middle-class girl who was. My mother accused the Head of English of racism and they came to an agreement that I could do A level English if I got a grade 1 in my Certificate of Secondary Education (CSE), which I managed to do.

Despite a few other setbacks and my head of year's insistence that I wasn't college material, I got a degree and a certificate in journalism.

I had no idea what was in store when I accepted a role on a newspaper in Worcestershire. Most of my colleagues were wonderful, but one freelancer's response, when I was racially abused in our office, was to say, 'I don't like her either, but I have to work with her.' This nearly sparked a strike by the National Union of Journalist members in our newspaper group, some of whom refused to work with him again. >

IT TOOK ME A WHILE TO REALIZE THAT SOME PEOPLE'S REACTION TO ME WAS DUE TO MY COLOUR

Despite being called 'the darky from *The Messenger*' to my face by the local criminals I covered in court, this was a brilliant job. I met some wonderful people, including my landlady, who I am still in touch with, and I had a great laugh with my fellow reporters.

I was also lucky that Jeff, my editor for most of the time, was scrupulously fair. I don't think either of the other two editors would have made me chief reporter. One joked about me using witchcraft and the other told me regularly that the readers hated me.

Yet nothing prepared me for the next phase of my career when I secured a place on the BBC's first training course for black and Asian television reporters. The course came about after the 1985 Brixton Riots, when it became blatantly clear that the BBC had very few black or Asian reporters.

Alas, the management failed to explain to their white journalists why the course was needed. Most colleagues were pleasant enough, but I experienced two years of backbiting and bullying by some journalists and camera crews, who lost no opportunity to let me know that I wasn't as good as the other news trainees and was only there because of my colour.

MOST COLLEAGUES WERE PLEASANT ENOUGH, BUT I EXPERIENCED TWO YEARS OF BACK-BITING

But my BBC experience paled into insignificance compared to my time at Yorkshire TV. Again, some colleagues were pleasant, but many others made me feel unwanted and out of place. One well-known presenter actually swore at me when I was producing a news bulletin with her, and a producer refused to cover the Leeds Carnival because 'it's just a bunch of darkies jumping up and down'.

I joined the Civil Service fourteen years ago, and although things seem fairer on the surface, the reality is that black and Asian colleagues are failing to progress. Black people are at the bottom, whereas white people are at the top. Yet I believe things are beginning to change.

Since George Floyd's murder, the head of our department has said that he doesn't want to preside over a racist organization. Senior leaders now have to sponsor and support black, Asian, and minority ethnic colleagues to progress. Some will do this because they have to, but I think a significant number genuinely believe it's the right thing to do. There is of course some pushback from white colleagues, but nevertheless I feel hopeful that things will be fairer for those who come behind me. To paraphrase Ben Lindsay, in his book, *We Need to Talk About Race*: I hope my ceiling will be their floor.

Sharrion J. Francis.
Civil servant.

Sharrion was born in Kingston, Jamaica, and grew up in London. A former print and TV journalist, she has a teenage son and is passionate about public service and social justice. She has been an independent visitor for looked-after children and is committed to mentoring youth.

AND BULLYING

BY SOME JOURNALISTS AND CAMERA CREWS

Lord Paul Boateng

THE RT HON THE LORD BOATENG
PC DL. MEMBER OF THE HOUSE OF LORDS

Sticks and Stones, or Mothers Preparing Children

'Sticks and Stones may break your bones, but words can never harm you.'

Nigger. Darkie. Wog.

Sticks and stones, sticks and stones.

Was he adopted? Is he yours? No. He is mine and yes, I am married to his father.

Why, Mummy? Why? They're just inquisitive, dear.

Sticks and stones. Sticks and stones. Growing up. Growing up.

Half-caste. Mixed race. Coloured.

Sticks and stones. Sticks and stones.

Why, Mummy? Why not there? Why?

Plenty of other places! They don't want your father, dear! So, I won't go!

Why, Mummy? Why? Ignorance, dear? Just ignorance! Pure ignorance!

Sticks and stones. Sticks and stones. Growing up. Growing up.

Strangers touching hair! So soft! So springy! How do you manage it?

Why, Mummy? Why do that? Why do they keep touching me? Why do they look at us so?

Because you're beautiful, dearest! So beautiful!

No dogs. No coloureds. No place. No jobs.

Because they know no better, dearest! Prejudice, dear! Pure prejudice!

Sticks and stones. Sticks and stones. Grown-up. Grown-up now.

STICKS AND STONES

And where do you come from? Hackney! No, where do you really come from?

Sticks and stones. Sticks and stones. Go home. Go home. Now.

When will it ever stop?

Such a beautiful accent! Where did you learn to speak like that? Why you speak English better than us!

Will it ever stop?

A graduate, a lawyer, a doctor, a politician, a . . . whatever!

Is that car yours? Do you really live on that road?

How come? Tell! Do tell! Did you ever? Have you ever? How come? Do tell!

'Sticks and stones may break your bones, but words can never harm you!'

But, Mummy, they do! It hurts! It hurts! It still hurts!

Yes, dear! But keep going, dear! Don't ever let it get to you!

You can be better than that! You can be better than them!

Hell, yes! I'm black! I can be better! Hell, no! Not better! The best!

The Rt Hon the Lord Boateng PC DL. Member of the House of Lords.

As a Member of Parliament, Baron Paul Boateng of Akyem and Wembley became Britain's first politician of African descent to serve as a Cabinet Minister. He was also the first black ambassador in British history when he was appointed High Commissioner to South Africa. Outside of politics, Lord Boateng is a Methodist lay preacher.

M. Jay

NEWS EDITOR AND
FILM-MAKER

M. Jay.
News editor and film-maker.

M. Jay grew up in Trinidad and Tobago,
surrounded by the arts and poetry. She was
a Presidential Scholar at Spelman College in
the USA, and also spent time in West Africa
as a Watson Fellow. In the UK, she has been
a journalist and film-maker, and currently
works in the field of diversity and inclusion.

WIP

Nomad
Traversing shores that flank
the Atlantic   across
Generations and within
lifetimes,   lifetimes
within

Potential squandered   detracted

ebbed but
buoyed   melanin
laced
dreams
of being

Herald and Harbinger
Reveries
Articulate perceptions both unifying
and estranging
Coveting parity

someday

M. Jay Gonzalez

Dotun Adebayo

RADIO PRESENTER, WRITER AND PUBLISHER

It's not personal, it's business. The moment I realized that, I was able to breathe a lot more easily.

It was a well-known presenter on one of the commercial radio stations that dropped the god-complex on me like, *Are you dumb or what?*

'What?' he whispered in my ear. 'You really thought I was going to say, "Yeah, Dotun, why don't you have my job?"'

I was horrified, but played it cool. It came out of nowhere. This bloke was supposed to be the right-on, politically correct face of the extremities of the 'dark side' of the radio dial/button/app. From a debate about the BBC's lack of black staff to a clarification from me that the only black folk I see at his commercial station are cleaners and security guards, to "Yeah, Dotun, why don't you have my job?" You really thought I was going to say that?' *Are you dumb or what?*

I won't lie. It grates on me when white guys make out like they're cleverer than black guys. Sometimes they are, but how were we to know that it wasn't personal? For literally hundreds of years we've been trying to figure out what it is that they've got against us. Done a lot of research myself, in those 'I guess that's why they call it the blues' moments, and I couldn't find anything in history that we did to them that makes them hate us so bad. But if it's not personal, and we don't have to take it personally, we can go about our business without the burden of discrimination that we carry with us everywhere, and which undoubtedly holds us back.

It's not personal. It's not because I am black. It's just because I'm not white.

That's a slightly less bitter pill to swallow. It makes no difference to the outcome. Discrimination is discrimination and the outcome is that we, who were made in the shade, get the sticky end of the stick. **>**

DISCRIMINATION
IS DISCRIMINATION

But at least I know it's more about them that it is about me. Somehow it feels like the joke's on them. They are discriminating against themselves. And that keeps me smiling.

But I am not dumb or what. Listening to the wisdom of Bob Marley, as I don't do nearly enough, I picked up some knowledge which has sustained me through one ah dem 'I guess that's why they call it the blues' moments. In an interview in the mid-1970s, when he was asked about the break-up of the original Wailers, with the departure of Bunny and Peter, Bob addressed the people who were hating on him, to bring it on, because their hate would only inspire a

great song: 'How do you think I write songs like "I Shot the Sherriff"? It was because o' the fight I was getting inna my own band.'

We get 'fight' every day. I used to think i was part of the black condition. That we were born warriors, not worriers. Now I know it's the white condition that brings it on, I'm more inclined to stand up strong ('*tallawah*') and lick it down with a rod of correction. Everybod' in business knows what a 'correction' is. It's language they understand. And remember this isn't like back in the day when it wa' personal and you threw your fists in a man' face because he called you the 'N word'. This ain't back in the day: there are laws agains' that kind of thing nowadays, so only a lunati'

I GUESS
THAT'S WHY THEY CALL IT
WHITE

walks up to your face and screams the 'N word' in it with all these iPhones and CCTV cameras about. Even at a football ground, they'll ban you for life. It's a lot more subtle than that these days. Today a man will look you in the face and *think* the N word. And you can see him thinking it: Are you (N words) dumb or what?

That's how come I can't reveal the name of this well-known presenter, who thinks that racial equality is all about his job. So subtle we may call him Salvador Dalì. He knows the rules of the racist game in a surreal world in which the goalposts have shifted from the personal to strictly business. But like I say, the correction . . .

Don't take it personal, Dotun. Salvador ain't got nothing against you personally. He's just fighting for his job using all the tools available to him. I guess that's why they call it 'white privilege'.

When I go on air I go into battle. Let Salvador's listeners decide who should have his job. It's not personal. Just business.

Dotun Adebayo MBE.
Radio presenter, writer and publisher.

Dotun was born in Nigeria. He is best known for his radio shows *Up All Night* and *Brief Lives* on BBC Radio 5. The publishing company, intentional Press, founded by Dotun, produced black fiction, including Patrick Augustus's *Baby Father* and Victor Headley's *Yardie*.

PRIVILEGE

Dawn Butler

MEMBER OF PARLIAMENT

It is difficult to describe the aftermath of George Floyd's brutal public murder in the United States. Or Breonna Taylor's. All I know is that it has brought up such generational trauma that it is exhausting.

I often feel laden by the weight of needless and mindless racism. I think I have done probably more than 200 meetings talking about Black Lives Matter in just a few months.

What has become so clear to me is just how important it is that we hold our allies close and dear. Our allies are vital, and this battle cannot be won without them.

I am a proud ally of the LGBTQI+ community, of those who are deaf, hard of hearing, and users of British Sign Language, of disabled people, and many more.

This not because of my personal circumstances. It is because I believe that everyone has a right to live as their true authentic selves, without being victimized, bullied, or discriminated against.

Until they get their equality, I can never truly get mine.

With allies, we will accelerate the path to justice, equality, and equity.

Just imagine what it is like being discriminated against over and over again, having systems designed to hold you back, to make you feel inferior. And having revealed the injustice, all one seeks is justice, not revenge. I hope that people globally can see the dignity and strength that is needed to do that.

I think about the shoulders on which I stand and I am encouraged to pursue a world without discrimination, and to try to ensure this is the last time black people have to fight this particular battle.

Race is a social construct that must be eliminated. Racism is the action that needs to be eradicated from every place, system, and structure in which it exists.

In the words of the inspirational freedom fighter and congressman John Lewis: 'Do not get lost in a sea of despair. Be hopeful, be

Racism is the action that needs to be eradicated from every place, system, and structure in which it exists

NEVER, EVER BE AFRAID TO MAKE SOME NOISE

optimistic. Our struggle is not the struggle of a day, a week, a month, or a year, it is the struggle of a lifetime. Never, ever be afraid to make some noise and get in good trouble, necessary trouble.'

He also said: 'And if we believe in the change we seek, then it is easy to commit to doing all we can, because the responsibility is ours alone to build a better society and a more peaceful world.'

So, I say to people – keep breathing, keep getting into good trouble, and together, we will see the change that we seek.

Dawn Butler.
Member of Parliament.

Dawn has been a Member of Parliament for Brent Central since 2015, and was named female MP of the year at the 2009 Women in Public Life Awards.

Ali Abdi BEM

YOUTH WORKER

AS I GREW UP,

I BECAME MORE AND MORE AWARE OF WHAT WAS HAPPENING IN

OUR SOCIETY

When we begin to lose our future generations and role models, instead we turn anger into action.

I am passionate about bringing people in my area into the community organizing process. We persuaded Nando's to open the first mainstream halal-compliant restaurant in Cardiff city centre; the community now see that change is possible if we act together with others for social justice and the common good.

My parents descend from Somaliland, East Africa – not to be confused with neighbouring war-torn Somalia – and came to Cardiff in the 1950s. My dad was a Merchant Navy seaman and travelled the world with other men from Somaliland. They did not see race nor colour as a dividing factor, and worked tirelessly to export coal and other stuff to port cities across the world. Many of them settled in Wales following their time at sea. As I grew up my father spent a lot of time

away, until the mid-1990s when an angina attack called time on his travels, and he spent the rest of the time helping my mother bring me and my siblings up. We all went to nursery and primary school in Grangetown, to Cathays for secondary education, and to a combination of universities in England and Wales.

I got into youth and community work shortly after high school in 2001, and since then I have noticed some of the smartest and most talented young men and women prevented, unconsciously or consciously, from reaching their full potential. As I grew up, I became more and more aware of what was happening in our society, and particularly the institutional racism that had prevented them from achieving their ambitions. At first, I was disheartened that, despite their academic achievements, young men and women of colour were not visible in public or in business, as managers or executives in our beautiful city of Cardiff. **>**

'Institutional racism, also known as systemic racism, is a form of racism that is embedded as normal practice within society or an organization. It can lead to such issues as discrimination in criminal justice, employment, housing, health care, political power, and education, among other issues' (*Oxford English Dictionary*).

I chose to turn my anger into action by joining Citizens UK and becoming a Community Organizer, with their Welsh chapter. Founded in October 2014, Citizens Cymru Wales builds diverse alliances of communities organizing for power, social justice, and the common good.

Our member organizations are churches, schools, mosques, unions, and other civil society organizations that have:

- Deep roots in their community;
- An interest in developing people to become effective community leaders;
- A vision for greater social justice;
- A willingness to turn that vision into action for the common good; and
- A hunger for change which local people can see, taste, or touch.

Over the last few years, I have launched and spearheaded the Community Jobs Compact, which aims to bring local people and employers together to tackle poverty, unemployment, and underrepresentation in the workforce, with an emphasis on employers committing to sign the Community Jobs Compact. This includes obligations to be accredited as a 'Living Wage for Wales' employer, to pay all staff and contractors at least £9.30 an hour, to recruit using name-blind and address-blind CVs, and/or guarantee an interview to local residents who meet the criteria, as well as introduce unconscious bias training for interviewers. The Compact will also ensure all staff have the option of a permanent contract, and demonstrate opportunities for growth and development; for instance, through internal career progression and mentoring.

We have successfully supported over 150 young people from BAME backgrounds into decent Living Wage jobs, with employers committed to equality, diversity, inclusion, and turning their vision into action and walking the walk. With employers like IKEA, ITV Wales, the Welsh Parliament, and housing associations, we are making strides to retain our most talented youngsters here in Wales, with businesses and organizations committed to their development.

My ambition for the future is to continue to tackle powerlessness in my community, as well as the frustration connected with it, and the perception that nothing can be done to overcome it. I have a strong track record of leading young people from Somali, BAME, and other disadvantaged backgrounds in non-partisan political action. Although there are many serious issues equally worthy of my attention and support, I derive the greatest pleasure from focusing on the challenges that my community is most anxious about.

My hope for Wales in the future is to help shape 'not the world as it is . . . but the world as it should be' (Finn Hudson, in *Glee*).

Ali Abdi BEM.
Youth worker.

Ali's work focuses on mentoring children in Cardiff schools to achieve academically, and to engage them in community organizing and leadership. Ali spearheaded and codeveloped a Community Jobs Compact, with the aim of bringing local people and employers together to tackle poverty, unemployment, and underrepresentation.

THERE ARE MANY SERIOUS ISSUES EQUALLY WORTHY OF MY ATTENTION AND SUPPORT. I DERIVE THE

GREATEST PLEASURE

FROM FOCUSING ON THE CHALLENGES THAT MY COMMUNITY IS MOST ANXIOUS ABOUT

Hermon and Heroda Berhane

FASHION AND TRAVEL BLOGGERS

Black, Deaf Women: Triple Oppression

R aised in our motherland, Eritrea, we both became deaf at the age of 7. We had to overcome the culture shock when we arrived in America and the UK. Within a hearing world, it can be lonely and frustrating.

Trapped.

We were told we wouldn't be able to achieve anything. Being black and deaf is a double struggle. We have to work ten times harder for any success we achieve. We have been overlooked for promotions, condescended to when attending fashion university, ignored at auditions, and insulted in our personal lives when out and about.

Trapped. **>**

NO
JUSTICE

As many black people growing up, we were raised in white culture. We felt that to succeed we had to abide by this culture to be taken seriously. All the time we would experience racism, micro-aggression and audism (audism is a form of discrimination aimed at deaf or hard-of-hearing people).

You don't see us, or you do but you're ignoring how we feel. People stare when we use sign language. We have lost count of the number of times people called us 'deaf and dumb'.

Trapped.

People feel sorry for us. We should get cured. In society, people say disability is a curse. We are always rejected by people. This is done in a passive way, but still hurts! So, people stop communicating and drift away because it is too hard to communicate.

For a black, deaf person in the UK, we see there isn't enough representation in the fashion, travel, theatres, TV, and film industries. Being black and deaf is not appealing enough. We're sick of it!

People need to do better, be more inclusive. We love travel, but they treat us differently because of our skin colour.

Being black is an oppression. Being a woman is an oppression. Being deaf is another oppression!

Trapped.

After the explosion of emotion and demands for action following the George Floyd incident, we were emotionally exhausted and tried to be strong constantly, but seeing so many images of pain and suffering each day is bound to affect us and you.

Still, we know it happened, as so many black lives were lost before George Floyd. We were praying that our black voices would be heard, and now the rest of the world has to wake up and see us. The world is crying out for equality and human rights, and the racists must be stopped. We cried, and our tears caused us to be exhausted.

We were at a peaceful BLM protest in Hyde Park with our friends, and people of all ages and from all different backgrounds screamed, 'No Justice, No Peace' – a sentiment that was echoed around the world.

It hurts saying their names over and over again: George Floyd, Breonna Taylor, Ahmaud Arbery, Stephen Lawrence, Mark Duggan, and so many more. But these protests gave us so much hope for the future. This was just the beginning of our fight against racism.

We are relieved the world woke up and listened to our pleas.

No more silence and no more feeling *trapped*!

Society will always try and push us aside, and we have to show them that we are not going to disappear. Being black, being deaf and being women is not a problem; it's society's attitude towards us that is the problem.

We started *Being Her* as a way to help black women with diversity, inclusion, and disability. We use social media to change misconceptions. We are very proud that we have managed to break down so many barriers. Our only disappointment is that there are so many barriers still left to break, and being black and deaf is *hard work*.

We are proud to be black and deaf. Being black and deaf gives us the strength and power that has made us the women we are today.

Hermon and Heroda Berhane.
Fashion and travel bloggers.

The model twins Hermon and Heroda Berhane have been breaking barriers in the fashion industry. Their Instagram page @being_her has a huge following. They have modelled for *Vogue* magazine and recently modelled for a new fashion campaign by River Island.

NO
PEACE

Ron Shillingford

PHOTOJOURNALIST AND AUTHOR

World's Longest Apprenticeship

'Anyone who writes for *The Observer* can write for us,' was the reassuring voice of the editor on the phone, whose oil magazine I was lined up to work for as their European correspondent. He made the next day's face-to-face interview sound like a mere formality. The only trouble was this plummy-voiced gatekeeper didn't realize he was teeing up a black man for his Arab paymasters.

I craved that job. I'd just had a double-page American football feature in *The Observer*'s Sunday supplement and, disillusioned with the glass ceiling of sports writing – the last bastion of the white male middle -class – had applied for this epic change of direction, working in London and the Middle East. Great package and prospects. Surely the gregarious Mr Plummy would hire solely on merit? After all, he'd confirmed the job was as good as mine.

The next day, when the receptionist phoned him announcing 'Mr Shillingford has arrived', a mix of emotions engulfed me: nerves, excitement, and a nagging resignation to the inevitable. Mr Plummy emerged and even though I was the only person in reception, he looked around for Ronald Shillingford. I shook my head. Here we go again. We went through the motions.

Same thing had happened at *Boxing News* a couple of years earlier. Through my enthusiasm and boxing knowledge on the phone, the editor of the sport's premier weekly publication promised in writing I'd be allowed to write about the burgeoning British scene, particularly on an outstanding heavyweight prospect, Frank Bruno. >

I SHOOK MY HEAD
HERE WE GO AGAIN

RACISM MADE IT HARDER

When I went in to confirm the job, the editor, with his best poker face, promised I could start, 'when the time is right', which was not what the letter stated. That day never materialized. A 17-year-old white kid got it instead.

English was the only subject I excelled at in school. Nevertheless, the careers master had zero interest in helping me: 'Do you know how good you need to be to be a journalist?'

His negativity spurred me on. After years of working in the black media, my big chance came in TV at *Trans World Sport* as an assistant producer. Interviewing Muhammad Ali was the highlight, as well as a trip to Detroit for a feature on the celebrated Kronk Boxing Gym. When recession hit in 1990 and five people were cut out of thirty, the only three black employees lost their jobs. And so back to *The Voice* I went.

There were scraps of TV and radio punditry, but no major opportunity emerged, even after the Macpherson Report in 1998 stated that every British industry is institutionally racist, including the media. As a knee-jerk reaction, the *Daily Mirror* raised my hopes, but within days they looked elsewhere for their token black appointee. Somebody else got it.

I ploughed on: wrote a novel (*No Glove No Love*), and a bestselling martial arts book (*The Elite Forces Handbook of Unarmed Combat*) – translated into Japanese and three other languages – and ghost-wrote Jamie Lawrence's biography (*From Prison to the Premiership*). They all raised my profile, but nothing came of them.

Caribbean Times, the weekly paper I edited, folded suddenly, just before Christmas 2006. In desperation, I applied to be sports editor at a daily paper in the Cayman Islands, 5,000 miles away. Success this time, but sadly I had to leave my wife and two young daughters behind in London. In Cayman, I published a series of sixteen ebook short stories, written from the perspective of white women. Highlights there included covering the 2010 Vancouver Winter Olympics and the London Olympics.

There were numerous attempts to find work back in London. Not a sausage. Thankfully, we defied the odds and our marriage survived over the next eight years, despite seeing loved ones for only a few weeks a year.

THAN ANTICIPATED AND I'VE OFTEN REGRETTED IT, BUT I RETAIN A POSITIVE OUTLOOK

Professionally, it hasn't been easy since returning to Blighty in 2016, but I'm still a resolute freelancer, I write biographies, and I hope to break through with *Maxathon*, my fitness workout, created to much acclaim in Grand Cayman. My TV comedy-drama scripts could take forever to be commissioned.

Meanwhile, the white journos I set out with have had long and lucrative spells in plum jobs in the media. Nevertheless, it's been a great ride. I entered journalism for a variety of reasons, but mainly to make a difference as a black man. Racism made it harder than anticipated and I've often regretted it, but I retain a positive outlook. It feels like the world's longest apprenticeship. At least Mr Plummy would admire my tenacity. And the careers teacher was evidently in the wrong job.

Ron Shillingford.
Photojournalist and author.

Ron studied civil engineering, but his main ambition was always journalism and publishing. His bestselling book *Elite Forces* has been translated into Japanese, Polish, Italian, and Russian. He has interviewed iconic figures, most notably Muhammad Ali.

Trevor Phillips OBE

WRITER, BROADCASTER
AND FORMER POLITICIAN

There are two lessons any person of colour, who hasn't forgotten who and what they are, will tell you about racism.

First, our parents came to a country whose winters were as cold as ice, and met people whose eyes seemed even colder. But they were proud men and women; too proud to beg people not to shout names at them or chase them down the street. Their answer was to show themselves to be as good as, even better, than anyone else. No black child escapes the lecture: 'In this place, you must work twice as hard to be half as successful.' Our parents knew that prejudice shrivels in the face of true worth.

Second, we each have our stories of slights and exclusions, even of insults or abuse. But whatever we endure today, those who came before suffered in a way that has left its mark. My great-great-grandfather was white. He was not my ancestor by my great-great-grandmother's choice. She survived and made it possible for her daughter to escape that fate.

Most of us carry on with our everyday lives, most of the time, without the humiliations, hurts, and terror that our ancestors endured. That doesn't mean that racism does not limit us or cause us pain. We remember things.

The invitation to a birthday party for the 'best' friend that mysteriously went astray. The rejection letter from the top university that admitted someone else with poorer grades last year. The job that we were invited to apply for, and we didn't even get an interview.

We swallow hard and carry on. But the bitter reality of racism for most of us is not one of random cruelty meted out by anonymous men in blue uniforms: it is of dreams denied, often by those we thought were friends and colleagues.

All the same, invited to think about racism,

WE
REMEMBER
THINGS

I'm not going to spend all my time dwelling on what others do to me, or fail to do for me. Personally, I prefer to think about how the life I make could be better than the life others want to prepare for me. I start with my tribe: seriously, nine brothers and sisters, from a mother who was one of four, and whose mother was one of eight, makes for a lot of cousins. They are my shield against the world; the elders gave me belief in us. I want to hand that on to those who come next.

I will also think about my friends and colleagues, none of whom want to judge me by what I look like; if they did, they wouldn't be friends or colleagues any more. My aim is to give them a reason to stand up for what's right – not to guilt-trip them or scare them into a show of anti-racism – but to help them persuade others that we will all be better people if we rid the world of prejudice.

And finally, I'll think about how I can ask my brothers and sisters of colour to stop beating on themselves and each other to be perfect. Yes, let's be honest with each other; we don't all have to agree about things – we're human after all. We think. We reason. We debate. But there are enough people only too keen to spell out our defects, so let's not join the crowd in pointing the finger at other people of colour.

Most of all, we can each make a difference by doing something positive for each other: a kind word, a kiss, a small favour.

The preacher had it right: in a world where we all struggle to see the right way forward, don't curse the darkness. Light a candle.

Trevor Phillips OBE.
Writer, broadcaster and former politician.

Trevor is a former chairman of the Equality and Human Rights Commission. Since 2015, he has been the President of the Partnership Council of the John Lewis Partnership.

Shaun Bailey

LONDON ASSEMBLY MEMBER

Sorrow, Anger, Determination

Race wasn't something I noticed in my very early years. It wasn't something I had to think about. Then one day, when I was X years old, I was chased by the National Front — and race suddenly came into my life.

Let me explain. I grew up in a council house in Ladbroke Grove. We were a big mix of nationalities, from Moroccans to Poles. But even though we looked like a Dulux colour palette, there was never really any racial tension. The colour of our skin just wasn't an issue.

That all changed for me when I went to visit my friend Gordon. He lived in a council house like mine, just at the top of my road. And as I turned the corner into his estate, a group of boys moved out of the shadows and identified themselves as members of the National Front. I was only vaguely aware of what that meant, but it became clearer a few seconds later when they started chasing me and threatening to kick my head in. Their taunts showed that, unlike my neighbours, they had a big problem with the colour of my skin.

So that was my introduction to racism. And ever since then, I've had to live with the knowledge that some people will dislike me because I'm black. All people of colour have this knowledge, and it's unsettling. It changes how you look at the world. More worryingly, it changes how you look at yourself.

Did teachers lower their expectations of me? Did I get turned down for this job because I'm black? Did this person ignore me because I'm black? You second-guess everything.

But second-guessing is sometimes better than being told outright. As I worked my way through politics, a calling that's supposed to represent our highest ideals, I had to deal with racism. I received letters and emails telling me to go back to my mud hut. The former Labour MP for my home borough, a white woman, called me a token ghetto boy. (I grew up in Ladbroke Grove. There was nothing token about it.)

The truth is racism takes many forms, and it's not confined to one group of people or political viewpoint. The far right tell us to go back to where we came from, not realizing that where we came from is normally just down the road. The far left want all people of colour to think and vote the same way; and if we dare to think for ourselves, then we're coconuts — or token ghetto boys.

It's upsetting. It's maddening. And in my early years, I found myself trapped in that cycle of sorrow and anger. But thanks to my mum, I started to understand that I could control my reaction to racism. That I didn't have to react in anger.

To this day, my mum tells me that living well is the best revenge. And she's right. Although our gut response to racism will always be sorrow and anger, we don't have to act on that sadness and anger. Instead, we can act with determination. Determination to prove the racists wrong. Determination to show our excellence. Determination to live well.

In part, that means living up to our potential. I was a youth worker for over twenty years, helping young people get out of gangs and into work. And I would hammer home this simple piece of advice: be excellent. We live in a society where we're increasingly judged by the content of our character, not by the colour of our skin. So, let's make sure we're proud of our characters. Every single one of us has potential; we just need to develop it.

On top of that, living well means seeking out the good people. Because although Britain might have racists, it's not a racist country. The vast majority of Brits are good people.

And on that note, I'd like to finish my story about the National Front. As I was being chased, I ran into Gordon and his brother – both white. Together, we stopped the National Front boys and told them to back off. I've never forgotten that. It's a reminder that everyone, of every colour, has a part to play. We can't create a more equal society by excluding white people from the conversation. So yes, let's keep working to defeat racism. But let's do it together, as one country.

Shaun Bailey.
London Assembly Member.

Shaun served as Prime Minister David Cameron's Special Advisor on Youth and Crime. He is a candidate for the 2021 London mayoral election.

Pat Younge

JOURNALIST AND CREATIVE LEADER

The Power of Memory

I remember the first time I was racially abused. I was about 6 and someone in the local park called me a 'wog' when I wouldn't let them join our football match.

I remember the girlfriend who wouldn't hold my hand in public because her family were National Front supporters. I also remember her older brother kicking the crap out of me when he found out about us.

I remember the family 'friend' who daubed the word 'sambo' in paint on the front wall of our council house.

I REMEMBER THE TEACHER WHO BRIDLED WHEN I CHALLENGED HIM, AFTER HE SAID EUROPEANS DISCOVERED AFRICA

I remember the countless times my hair and skin were treated like a petting zoo.

I remember the kids who threw stones at me and called me 'nigger', when I went to collect my brother from infant school.

I remember the teacher who bridled when I challenged him after he said Europeans discovered Africa.

I remember scanning the layouts of unfamiliar pubs to make sure I knew where my exit routes were, in case someone kicked off at me.   **>**

I KEEP
MOVING
FORWARDS

I remember the excessive scrutiny I experience at passport control. Everywhere. All the time.

I remember being butt of the dick jokes in the cricket and rugby dressing rooms, and I remember being introduced to the word 'banter' and advised not to get a chip on my shoulder.

I remember the women who clutch their handbags that bit tighter when I'm near them, imperceptible to most, but not to me.

I remember every time I open a video on Facebook that I might watch an African-American male die.

I remember looking at the Cardiff University rugby team sheet, on the wall outside the Athletic Union office, where my name had been crossed out and someone had written 'Blacktrick Younge'.

I remember the neighbour who racially abused my mother across the front gardens.

Some of these things happened decades ago, yet I remember all of them – and hundreds of incidents like them – as if they happened yesterday.

But . . .

I also remember my mother telling me from my earliest days, that if a white candidate for a job had nine qualifications, I would need to have ten.

I also remember her telling me not to waste my time trying to make racists like me, and instead, spend my energy making sure they couldn't stop me pursuing my dreams.

I also remember the love of the overwhelming majority of white people who took me and my family for who we were. I remember some of them ignored pressure to shun us from their families and peers, choosing instead to befriend us, and even go into battle with us and for us.

I also remember the inspiration of Ali, Pele, Viv, Daley, Cyril, Brendan, and Laurie, who showed we could excel on the field of play . . . and do it our way.

I also remember the first time a black man

I'd never met nodded at me as we passed in the street, and how I felt empowered and no longer alone.

I also remember educating myself on our history and culture, reading Martin,

BECAUSE EVERY DAY I WAKE UP AND REMEMBER MY LIFE

Malcolm, Alex, Chinua, Maya, Toni, Alice, Steve, James, Angela, CLR, and Nelson, and expanding my vision of what was possible through their stories and struggles.

I also remember learning the hard way which battles to fight and which slights to ignore, refusing to conform to other people's stereotypes or expectations of who I could be, or what I could become.

I also remember Kelso, Stephen, Roland, the New Cross 13, Joy, Cynthia, Colin, and all the others we lost too soon.

I also remember losing myself in the sounds from other worlds through the Jackson 5, Motown, Marvin, Aretha, Diane, and Bob, and then finding my own voice, in the lyrics of our world, through the Specials, Steel Pulse, Heatwave, and Soul II Soul.

I also remember a time when we were all black, and the power of that collective political stance against racism and racial discrimination.

I keep moving forwards because every day I wake up and remember my life, in this place and at this time, was not supposed to happen. I remember that when my ancestors were taken in chains and subjected to the brutality of the middle passage and life in bondage on the plantation, that this was not part of the plan.

I remember that I, where I am today, and where I may be tomorrow, was never the plan for those who enslaved us.

I remember I'm here today because of the fortitude, resilience, courage and wisdom of my forebears, most of them unrecorded, unnamed and unknown.

It is because I remember how many people have suffered and had dreams denied to make me possible – in this moment, in this time, and in this place – that I've committed myself to taking the opportunity that my life represents and to seize it with both hands. That's the power of memory. Never forget.

Pat Younge.
Journalist and creative leader.

Pat has three decades of experience working in news, sport, commissioning and production across ITV, BBC and Channel 4. He is a cofounder and co-managing director at Cardiff Productions Ltd. Pat is a digital enthusiast; his *Hack The Moon* documentary was nominated for a Webby Award.

Patrick
Vernon OBE

SOCIAL COMMENTATOR
AND ACTIVIST

Our Parents Did: Ode to the Windrush Generation

I wrote this poem during the height of the Windrush Scandal, around June 2018, after attending and speaking at the Windrush Scandal march and demonstration in Nottingham. We chanted 'Our parents did', recognizing our contribution to Britain and the failure of the Government to resolve the scandal. I built the chant into a poem to capture the significant contribution of African and Caribbean elders and their children, who migrated to Britain as part of the Windrush Generation. This poem has gone down well at numerous events over the last two years when I shared it at various public gatherings – gala dinner functions, Windrush Day events, and Black Lives Matter rallies. I read this at the funeral in September 2020, in Wolverhampton, of Paulette Wilson, who died connected to the hostile environment as a Windrush campaigner.

Who worked in the factories, mines and in manufacturing? Our Parents Did

Who worked on the buses? Our Parents Did

Who built the NHS? Our Parents Did

Who worked in care and nursing homes? Our Parents Did?

Who brought Pentecostalism, gospel music and Rastafari? Our Parents Did

Who performed in football, cricket, martial arts, athletics and elite sports at national and international level? Our Parents Did

Who brought rice and peas, ackee and saltfish and jerk chicken? Jollof rice, fufu.

Our Parents Did

Who brought pardner? Our Parents Did

Who brought Ujima economics, Kwanza and self-help? Our Parents Did

Who worked in retail and catering? Our Parents Did

Who brought ska, dub, reggae, lovers rock, soca, calypso, Brit funk, Afrobeat, highlife? Our Parents Did

Who brought blues parties, and sound systems? Our Parents Did

Who brought fashion and style, barber shops and hot combs? Our Parents Did

Who worked for the Council? Our Parents Did

Who worked in education, learning and academia? Our Parents did

Who worked in the armed forces? Our Parents did

Who worked for the Police? Our Parents did

Who ran businesses? Our Parents Did

Who got elected, campaigned, lobbied, marched, protested and agitated for our rights? Our Parents Did

Who laid the foundation for black Britons today? Our Parents Did? Our Parents Did.

Patrick Vernon OBE.
Social commentator and activist.

Patrick is a British social commentator and Windrush Campaigner of Jamaican heritage. He is a former councillor for the London Borough of Hackney. He is also a DJ and board game inventor.

Nadine White

JOURNALIST

Like many other journalists, I am glued to Twitter in between deadlines and I saw when the clip of George Floyd's murder first went viral.

I knew that I'd have to view the footage to ascertain the facts, as this news was dominating the headlines.

But I grappled with the prospect of being traumatized by watching it. For me, that's a constant reality, particularly in my line of work, where I cover racism often.

After a few hours, I pressed 'play' and made it to about three minutes in before I just couldn't sit through any more; I understood enough by then. When I looked at George, I saw every black person I've ever loved and it hurt to my core.

The painful legacy of racism affects my very being.

Poet Mutabaruka once said, 'Slavery isn't black history, slavery interrupted black history.' I bear the surname of the European man who enslaved my ancestors and branded them as his property.

Due to the disruption of slavery, which continues to reverberate across generations, and the resounding absence of detailed information relating to African heritage, I do not know my family history beyond that point. What does that do to a person who yearns for deep knowledge of self?

With every article I write about racism, there's guaranteed to be a handful of online trolls pointing out some irony of my being black and highlighting racism yet having the surname 'White'. Original.

But I have long resolved to wear the name in unashamed reappropriation of what was once disparaging and ambiguous, while making efforts to piece together as much information as possible about my family history. In addition to this, I enthusiastically soak up my own present-day experiences, which also make me the person that I am. I'm writing my chronicles, honey. >

WITH EVERY ARTICLE I WRITE ABOUT RACISM, THERE'S GUARANTEED TO BE A HANDFUL OF ONLINE TROLLS

With that said, I recently did some research into my lineage and understand I descend from West Africans who were based in Jamaica; most of the runaway slaves on the island, in the 1700s and 1800s, were from this region of the continent.

Fast-forward a couple of centuries to postmodern Britain. I'm a second-generation descendant of the Windrush Generation who were invited here to rebuild the country by the post-war British Government as Commonwealth subjects – and treated so appallingly by xenophobic racists. Then later gut-punched by the very same Government through the recent Windrush Scandal once they had served their purpose.

And, in one way or another, my family members' experiences as unwelcome migrants shaped the trajectory of their lives for better and for worse.

Then, of course, I came along – spiritually moulded by these experiences long before I even realized it.

My first, direct experience of racism happened in 1999, aged 7, when a white boy called me the N word in the playground. I'd never heard it before, but automatically felt *othered* and instinctively knew that this was his intention.

My usual experiences of racism have manifested within educational or corporate institutions, as opposed to, say, on the street. That's the British way: racism here is embedded in institutions and a lot more covert than other places.

I went to a predominantly white secondary school where I faced daily micro-aggressions and stuck out like a sore thumb.

University was the same, as well as much of the training and work experiences that I have undertaken thereafter, barring a few.

In addition to my anglicized name, I also took to anglicizing the contents of my CV in order to secure media job interviews, which worked a treat. But when I turned up, I would often see the visible shock on interviewers' faces to see a black girl standing in front of them. One snooty white woman was so affronted that she point-blank refused to shake my hand.

Naturally these experiences served to knock my confidence. It taught me to quieten my voice and shrink myself to be palatable.

But my innate desire to see a fairer world means that I align myself with the cause of anti-racism in all forms and, in furtherance of this, commit to amplifying black perspectives across the national news agenda as part of my vocation. I do this within an industry where only 0.2 per cent of journalists are black.

It has taken years of work to get back to being the daring 7-year-old prior to the utterance of that abhorrent word. And now that I have found my voice – I can't ever go back to being silent again.

Nadine White.
Journalist.

Nadine covers current affairs, race, and social justice for HuffPost UK. She is an Amnesty UK Media Award finalist.

IT HAS TAKEN YEARS OF WORK TO GET BACK TO BEING THE DARING SEVEN-YEAR-OLD PRIOR TO THE UTTERANCE OF THAT ABHORRENT WORD

Vaughan Gething

MEMBER OF THE
WELSH ASSEMBLY GOVERNMENT

I have had a good life and I look forward to many more good years. I had a loving family growing up, good friends, and a supportive school environment. My family stood out though. In my village school the only non-white children were my family. In high school my family were at least half of the non-white children. I visited that school a few years ago and the mix hadn't changed.

I didn't feel different for most of my life growing up. I still wanted the West Indies to succeed and was especially interested in successful black figures, without ever thinking about it. Racism was a minor intrusion and just something to deal with. It hurt when it happened, but it was only as I got into teenage years that I realized how different I was and how some people treated me on sight. >

Fast-forward several decades and I'm a husband, dad, and public figure. I think about our son and his future.

A few years ago we went to America. It was an amazing trip, taking in New Orleans, Nashville, and Memphis. I

IT'S THE FUTURE

wouldn't go on that trip today. I'd be too worried about getting stopped in the hire car, or on the street. I wouldn't want to expose myself or my family to that risk. America has gone backwards, but here in Wales, we have our own problems too.

I will need to prepare my son for the challenges that he will face. When do I talk to him about the language some people might use about me or him, or about how some people will look differently at him? That is something that's still hard to explain. All of us who aren't white know about the look you get when people wonder who you are, why you're there, and where you're from. It isn't a compliment. I don't think most people understand what it's like to be black and to be expected to justify our entitlement to be normal.

I'm optimistic about my son's future, but I know that he will face racism in his life. It's hard to accept, even though I know it's true. We will make sure that he knows he never has to ask permission to belong in his own country. He will never have to sacrifice who

he is – Irish, Zambian, and of course, Welsh.

The bigger challenge is changing other people's problems being projected onto him, me, and the rest of us. It isn't as easy or simple as making a speech on racism or celebrating Black History Month. If only changing hearts and mind were that simple. I think some of us got comfortable and complacent with progress. Positive progress is not inevitable – it happens because we will it, because we act to make a difference.

I don't have a perfect answer. I still believe change comes from leadership and from community experience and action. Our leadership is challenged and contradictory across the UK. The progress in terms of the UK Cabinet make-up is compromised by the nativist appeals to prejudice that the current Prime Minister has made and never apologized for. That matters because it gives licence to prejudice.

In Wales our curriculum reforms include embedded black experience as part of the history and future of Wales, and is an important example of national leadership,

THAT MATTERS AND I AM STILL AN OPTIMIST ABOUT WHAT WE CAN AND WILL DO

to reflect who we are, and crucially, who we want to be as a nation. It's not just important to me as a politician – it's much more important to me when I look at my family. It really isn't just my son who needs to know that this is his country, that our history is imperfect and complicated. His classmates, future workmates, future team mates, and all the people who he will never meet should be part of that conversation. It's only one part of what we should be doing as a country in changing and opening up the lived experience of families across our country.

My son should be less likely to be verbally abused on a night out or on a sporting pitch, less likely to be refused to be considered for a job, less likely to be asked by the police what he's doing when he's waiting for a bus at a bus stop. All of those things and more happened to me. Much worse has happened to others, and could still happen in the future. But it's the future that matters and I am still an optimist about what we can and will do.

Vaughan Gething.
Member of the Welsh Assembly Government.
Vaughan has served as Minister for Health and Social Services since 2016, and has served as Member of the Senedd for Cardiff South and Penarth since 2011. Vaughan graduated as a lawyer and was the first black president of the National Union of Students, Wales.

David Lammy

MEMBER OF PARLIAMENT

'Dear Wog. I have just been made aware of the extremely rude and disrespectful remarks you have made about Ann Widdecombe's speech at the EU recently. You should be hung upside down, suspended by your dirty black bollocks and given a severe thrashing. Now get yourself a banana and climb back up your tree. Sink the *Windrush*, its cargo of filth.'

2016 to 2019 was particularly intense. I had made several interventions that had been swept up by the news cycle, one of which was calling for a second referendum on the UK's departure from the EU. It's understandable that this fuelled a fiery debate over the legitimacy of a second referendum, but it also acted as a siren's call for white supremacists, hatemongers, and xenophobes. Speaking out against a project that had been co-opted by the far right gave those it emboldened the confidence to try and silence me.

'Mr black person . . . You are not English. You have to be white to be English and you are unfortunately black. So, why don't you fuck off to the shithole you crawled out of. Scum. Make England white again.'

When people call for me to go back to where I came from, I presume they don't mean Tottenham, where I was born and raised. They mean Guyana, the birthplace of my parents, who both came to the UK as part of the Windrush Generation.

After my father walked out when I was just a child, my mother raised me and my siblings by herself. She worked three jobs to make sure there was enough food on the table, and so all of her children could afford to go on school trips. For all my mother's outward strength, she was shy and reticent. Even as a young boy, I could tell she was nervous around white authority figures – teachers, doctors, and the police. I watched them belittle her and mock her accent. I remember most vividly the time she went to register the birth of my little sister, and the staff cruelly mimicked her pronunciation and the spelling of her new daughter's name.

It is my mother who I thank for the blessed position I am now in as a Member of

THAT GIVES ME COURAGE

Parliament. And it is her memory that gives me the courage to persevere in the face of hatred.

More deeply, the racist bile I receive simply reminds me of what I'm fighting for as a parliamentarian. I'm fighting for a society free of the kind of discrimination that my mother faced, and that my constituents continue to face to this day.

When it comes to discrimination and prejudice, the kind of explicit racist abuse I receive barely scratches the surface. Often, when people think of racism or white supremacy, they think of angry white men waving St George's flag, or skinheads waving torches. **>**

The truth is that white supremacy is much bigger than individual racists. It's a system where black lives matter less. It's a system where the instruments of power are controlled by white people – 97 per cent of Britain's elite is controlled by white people. Just 36 of 1,000 of the UK's top political, judicial, financial, cultural, and security roles are held by ethnic minorities. Black unemployment is at 9 per cent compared to the 4 per cent average. There is a 13 per cent

are still forced to overcome. More importantly, it is a reminder of the responsibility I bear to tear them down.

The racists are loud, and it can often feel overwhelming. However, in my experience, the vast majority of ordinary people are kind, compassionate, and decent, and they go out of their way to get past discrimination. I have had many mentors, teachers, and idols who inspire

IT SIMPLY
REAFFIRMS

attainment gap between black and white students at university.

The racism I have experienced throughout my life is a reminder not just of the small pockets of hatred that exist in our society, but of the deep racial inequalities that lie underneath. It is a reminder of the deprived circumstances I grew up in as a child in Tottenham. And it is a reminder of the barriers to opportunity my constituents

me with their openness and readiness to not only speak for anti-racism, equality, and justice, but live it too. This is why racist abuse won't silence or scare me. It simply reaffirms the importance of speaking out against the structures that generate it. In refusing to be silenced by systemic racism, hopefully I can empower others to join me in resistance.

THE IMPORTANCE OF SPEAKING OUT

David Lammy.
Member of Parliament

David is a qualified barrister. He led the campaign for Windrush British citizens, forcing the Home Secretary to guarantee the citizenship of Commonwealth nationals. He is the first black Briton to study for a Masters in Law at Harvard Law School.

Marcia Degia

FOUNDER AND PUBLISHING EDITOR
OF KOL SOCIAL

A Life Exhausted

I was born exhausted. Caught in the middle of someone else's seismic physical hell, my limbs weighed down by the amniotic fluids I swallowed. The joined bodies of mother and child now split apart as air viciously jabbed my scalloped lungs. I couldn't breathe.

The new parents, Caribbean-born, were already trapped in a racially divided foxhole. I was, after all, a Martin Luther King baby, thrust into the world almost nine months to the day after Dr King's April- 1968 murder. One could almost say that my conception preordained a career in the media.

Disillusioned after some twenty years in the industry, I founded a publication that tries to address the concerns of the excluded, underrepresented, misrepresented, and mistreated. A voice for those who strive to be heard. In 2019, *KOL Social* magazine was born tired.

Despite all the laws, activism, politics, and progressive endeavours, the cat-and-mouse games still play out and we are still being killed. And by 'killed' I mean physically, spiritually, and economically, amid a proliferation in the numbers of far-right racist groups. Here we are, more than fifty years on from the somewhat predictable assassination of the great American Civil Rights, icon and it's the same old. The world over, black men and women continue to die, attacked by police and vigilantes – a sad state of affairs that the killing of George Floyd in the summer of 2020 brought to the fore with a vengeance.

There have of course been countless antiracism protests in the past, but the 2020 global wave of demonstrations was different. Floyd's murder was really the first time that unlawful police aggression leading to the death of a black person had been clearly and graphically captured on film. In the ensuing outrage that exploded across the world it was instantly clear to me what my role was to be – as friends and allies took to the streets to protest, I chose words as my method of activism.

I began to type, compelled to sit at my computer and feverishly churn out one news story after another, trying obsessively to reach out to as wide an audience as possible. Then, as if I'd beaten out a silent drum message to the universe, people began to send me the tools and resources to continue along this path. Friends, colleagues, family, and even people I had never met, reached out.

Hour by hour, news stories assailed my inbox. Seasoned photographers and passionate protesters sent streams of powerful images. Eagle-eyed social media followers passed on floods of information that they felt warranted a platform. The content was racially diverse, with many non-black ethnicities standing with black activists and telling their stories. My fingertips at times went numb from all the continuous typing. But despite the frenetic pace, the collective spirit fuelled my resolve.

By the end of the summer, I was shattered. Worn out by each reignited bout of anger that took hold with every unfolding event, or whenever further aspects of ingrained systemic racism revealed themselves.

Dead tired answering the same old questions hurled at me from both the ignorant and those paralysed by white guilt:

'No, all protestors are not violent looters.'

'Yes, I think it's time to retire the Aunt-Jemima packaging.'

'No, I don't think they should ban *Gone with the Wind*.'

'Which colonial statue?'

Towards the end of his life, and definitely as the final breaths were being forced from his lungs on account of the white knee parked on his neck, I imagine that George Floyd, like many of us, was pretty exhausted.

Marcia Degia.
Founder and publishing editor of *KOL Social*.

KOL Social is a quarterly publication committed to sharing the experiences and perspectives of black, Asian, and ethnic groups from around the world. Marcia has worked for more than twenty years in print journalism and television. Former positions include acting managing editor of *Homes & Gardens*, publisher at Macmillan, and editor of *Pride Magazine*, for women of colour.

Bonnie Greer OBE

PLAYWRIGHT, THEATRE
CRITIC AND SOCIAL
COMMENTATOR

A Descendant of Transcendence

I have recently realized, through the attention and loving care of a person dear to me, that I have been an artist all my life.

Thing is, I made theatre before I had seen any.

Drew, painted on my mom's brown shopping bags in which she used to bring home groceries.

Watched vintage Hollywood movies and loved European cinema. I wrote my own versions.

I can tell you a lot about Truffaut and Fassbinder.

At about 10, I announced in my catechism class, in my Roman Catholic school, that I understood the Holy Trinity: how God could be three-in-one.

I pointed out that water could be three-in-one – solid; vapour, liquid – and still be water. >

My teacher told me, in a loud voice, that it was not possible for me to understand because 'the Holy Trinity is a mystery!'

It being a Friday, we went to the school hall to see a movie.

This one was a Tarzan flick featuring people who looked like me, running around, screaming, and bug-eyed, putting people into cooking pots with Cheetah, the fabulous chimpanzee, observing it all from a high tree.

This was an elite education for a black girl (called 'Negro') in the late 1950s and early 1960s in the USA, in what was called 'the ghetto'.

I knew that I was lucky that our dad worked six nights a week at the can-making factory to pay for our fees, books, uniforms, bus money, and lunches.

Problem was that I knew and saw no girls like me who did the things that I wanted to do.

Being a teenager in the late 1960s and especially 1968, I did all of the proper activist things except participate in burning down my own community and chucking rocks at the police.

Too politely brought up to do any of that.

But I cut my hair short and wore it in its natural state, which I have done ever since, and tried to find a way to express myself and be present for the community.

Sometimes these things conflicted.

They still do.

Racism for me was a given.

It was the built-in assumption about my intelligence, intention, goals, and destiny.

It took a long time to see and understand this because I built defence mechanisms.

In order to stay alive.

As me.

Unfortunately, I learnt to be careful about some fellow black people, too, because we can internalize racism and spit it out as class distinction, nationalism, and gender.

I am old enough to have seen every movement and nothing now is new, just packaged differently and with different slogans.

IF I AM LUCKY
TO HAVE A
DEATH BED

Because what racism does is infantilize.

Never allows growth and maturity. No past achievements.

Racism only entitles youth.

Maturity implies history, continuity, memory.

Racism mainly, like slavery was, is about erasure.

This is the number one enemy of people of colour, but it is hard to tell this to young people. Sometimes the best thing to do is let them find out things on their own.

I had to find out things, too.

Right now, for me is about the elimination of erasure and it does not bother me at all what price I pay to do this.

Because the child of Erasure is Fantasy.

'Wakanda' was invented by a white cartoonist.

He was not thinking of me.

I cannot say that I am hopeful for the future in the sense that you can put that phrase on some greeting card.

But I come from a people who decided to live and not die, so that is my credo and my light.

Every day is strong and good.

I learn a lot.

If I am lucky to have a death bed, I will be learning there, too.

Being what Wynton Marsalis said about his late father, the great Ellis Marsalis. who died of Covid-19: 'He went out of life like he lived: facing reality.'

Not here for sentiment.

Nor politics in a formal sense.

Everything political now anyway is a variation on the activity and causes of my youth.

This is hard to say and to face: but real change takes a long time.

The system is built to absorb change.

You must get older, live some, to see this.

But if your ancestors were sold into slavery, forced on to a boat towards what must have seemed to them to be oblivion, then you are this:

A Descendant of Transcendence.

Be it.

Bonnie Greer OBE.
Playwright, theatre critic and social commentator.

Bonnie was born in America, and is the winner of the Verity Bargate Award for Best New Play. She is on the board of a number of leading arts organizations, including the British Museum, the Royal Opera House, and the London Film School. She is a regular contributor to BBC2's *Newsnight*.

I WILL BE
LEARNING THERE, TOO

'Give someone a fish,
they'll eat for a day.
Teach them how to fish,
they'll eat forever.'

AFRICAN PROVERB

Part IV
Looking Out, Growing in Strength

Pam Wrigley

Dean Alexander

Dr Faith Uwadiae

Chef Orlando

Shereener Browne

Allan Willmot

Kayisha Payne

Ray Emmet Brown

Diana Dahlia

Albert Amankona

Kaya Lockiby-Belgrave

Brendon Winter

Jackee Holder

Andrea E. L. Attipoe

Sonia Campbell

Kevin Maxwell

Professor Uzo Iwobi

Bernadette Thompson

Dr Sarah Essilfie-Quaye

Pam Wrigley

BUSINESSWOMAN

It started with a trip down Memory Lane. We are planning a school reunion: fifty members of a new WhatsApp group, posting photos and sharing memories forty years after leaving the Hume Grammar School for Girls in Oldham. The conversation thread moved to bands we went to see, and one simple comment about Madness took me down the path I had pushed deep down inside.

I too had a ticket to see the band, but after weeks of internal anxiety I had decided not to go.

Madness had a big National Front and skinhead following in the 1970s and I knew I would not be safe. I sold my ticket, making excuses about not being able to go, and I felt a weight lifted off my shoulders. I hadn't told anyone the reason why until today.

For the first time I explained to my friends why I had decided not to go, then I remembered being spat at on the streets, the jeers of 'nigger' if I got on the bus when I was alone. As awful as it was, the safest thing for me was to stay on the bus and soak up the taunts until I got to my bus stop, so at least I would be near home. I recalled one of the popular boys at school offering to take someone 'out' after he overheard a six-foot guy mutter 'nigger' under his breath at me, as we walked into a crowded house party.

All these memories had been lost in time, but clearly not forgotten. Memories of the injustices of my teenage years flooded back as the WhatsApp conversation continued and they overwhelmed me. At the end of the day, I was emotionally drained.

I kept quiet in the 1970s and early 1980s at school, about what happened to me on a regular basis, because no one could do anything.

My solace and support also came unequivocally from white people and these negative events were way outnumbered by the open-minded, supportive, helpful people who helped me grow into the person I am today. >

I was born into a white family in the early 1960s, near Saddleworth Moor, the result of a passionate, extramarital affair. I've been told the midwife announced, 'Look what the coal man's brought,' as she handed me to my mum, the fourth of four girls. I never knew my biological father and I don't need to know.

I was welcomed and embraced with love and adoration by my mum, dad, and sisters, and so, my love, nurture, and sense of self-worth came from my white family. Moreover, I was accepted by my extended white family. No questions were asked: I was Pam, and I was loved and treated equally.

I gained a scholarship to the local grammar school and it was like a safe haven. When I walked through the school gates, the taunting and jeering would stop. My safety at school was ensured by the 100 per cent white teachers and my 97 per cent white classmates.

Now, forty years later, I feel heard by my classmates who were totally unaware of what was happening outside the school gates. Their eyes have been opened and that's a start.

I was lucky: my family were unerring in their support for me and along with school, they combined to make me feel I could do anything in life. My family can never walk in my shoes, but their footprint makes a mark in the ground beside mine. Their love sits deep in my heart and surrounds me, and I move in the world with a sense of belonging and with deep connections with people of all creeds and colours. Strangely enough, the biggest thing I felt holding me back was being working class. I left my northern, working-class roots behind to move to London, where I am simply seen as a northerner.

In comparison to a northern mill town, in London everyone is different and the whole world blends and melds, and no one stands out.

I've found my niche in the world, happy with who I am, and with a positive, open heart. I feel equal to everyone, even though in some eyes I am not black enough, and in others I am seen only as black.

So, I stride forth, believing in myself and knowing I belong in the world. And it's a great place to be.

Pam Wrigley.
Businesswoman.
Pam is the founder of Create Beautiful Hair, and has worked exclusively in the wedding industry for over twenty-five years, winning several industry awards; most recently, Wedding Hair Specialist 2020 and

I'VE FOUND MY NICHE IN THE WORLD, HAPPY WITH WHO I AM, AND WITH A POSITIVE, OPEN HEART

Dean Alexander

STYLIST AND
CREATIVE DIRECTOR

The Art of Progress

I am a creative visionary who believes that you must never compromise your core principles. Being black in the UK definitely has its challenges. You will find that you are not only competing with a biased society, submerged in systemic racism and prejudices, but you also have to navigate the snares and pitfalls of your own people. Sometimes it is much easier to accept the thirty pieces of silver.

On reflection, I guess I have been pretty lucky. Despite being born in England, I escaped the psychological effects of racism. I am not saying living in this society where racism exists has not made my road to accomplishment more difficult; even stemming the full potential of what, otherwise, could have been greatness to mere mediocrity. But I have never allowed myself to fall victim, or to be sentenced to the prison of mental slavery. Your understanding of the origins, customs, and journey of your people is important to the comprehension of how you truly live in a diaspora and not just survive in it.

At a very early age, I moved to the Caribbean with my grandmother, and this experience allowed me to understand the importance of controlling your own destiny. Growing up on an island where the primary focus was education and achieving, my observation of black people in prominent positions conditioned my mindset to the fact that my skin colour was not a barrier.

I was fortunate to attend an elite grammar school, which produced many great graduates, including prime ministers, world-renowned sportsmen, and artists, so my standards were always high from a young age. We were taught not to feel inferior and the educational system was progressive not restrictive. Learning black history in the Caribbean was also very important in helping me to understand my heritage. This foundation was instrumental in developing my inner drive that helps me to accomplish many of the things I do.

Returning to England in the late 1980s was a bit of a culture shock, to say the least: although I had encountered social class prejudice, racism was a new experience. I remember my first experiences of racism left me quite puzzled and then angry. Most of it came from the police: being stopped, and harassed almost weekly, and sometimes arrested for just driving a nice car.

In my work I encountered obstacles when I did certain projects, I always had to go the extra mile unlike my white counterparts, but my upbringing kept me strong and resolute. I created my own path. I knew that in a country where the framework for racism was invented, we must learn to be self-reliant while integrating. Why would you ask a system that oppresses you to help you to progress?

Running an awards ceremony (Movie Video and Screen Awards) that recognizes people of colour in film and television has revealed to me some of the institutionalized obstacles that makes it difficult for black people. Although the ceremony rivals any other in the UK and is supported by many actors and industry personnel, fourteen years later we still struggle to get proper television coverage. Go figure!

I believe the inequality begins in the early education system, designed not to advance our black children, but rather to cultivate de-education, creating a system of disenfranchisement condemning black youths to a social underclass. The killing of George Floyd in the USA shone a spotlight on racial injustices here in the UK, forcing our Government into addressing racial inequalities. But let us not be fooled! Remember the Windrush Scandal? Every time there is a crisis or atrocity against the black community the political and corporate spin doctors go into action, deploying damage-control measures. Black people are then the key focus for that season.

If we do not build together, we will never break free from this oppressive cycle. We must bake our own loaf of bread and not wait for crumbs from others. Ten years ago I started the Black Pound Day to encourage commerce within the black community. It is great to see its resurgence once again. but we must learn that the fight for equality is not for a season but a lifetime and generational. We must also police the images that are used to portray us and always remember, the aim of progress is never to use the past as a place of refuge, but as a point of reference.

Dean Alexander.
Radio broadcaster and producer.

Dean is the founder and director of the Movie Video and Screen Awards. The awards celebrate the work of black creatives in the television and film industry. As a radio presenter, Dean has hosted breakfast and drive-time slots and his own four-hour specialist show. He has a strong background in event management, computing, and user interface design.

Dr Faith
Uwadiae

IMMUNOLOGIST

Work twice as hard for half as much.' This is a phrase that many black children are told from an early age. The concept that because of your skin colour, you will be treated worse, and will have to work harder at every stage of your life to achieve your goals.

This is not a phrase that I grew up with. I was brought up in London, in a Nigerian household, to the phrases 'Education, Education, Education', 'Hard work pays', and Don't be an NFA' (i.e. don't be someone with No Future Ambitions – NFA).

Basically, my immigrant parents instilled into me the idea that if you worked hard and believed in yourself, you could achieve anything. These beliefs shaped my early life and I lived by these concepts. I put my head in my books and ground my way through my GCSEs and A levels. I was the epitome of a teacher's pet and I largely got through by following my passion for science resiliently. My goal was to finish school, go to university, get a great job, and no longer be poor. If I worked enough, the world would be my oyster, right? What I am trying to say is I bought into the idea of meritocracy.

However, I was not completely naive. I knew from the news that black people were treated badly in this country, but when I was young, racism to me was overt. Racism was the existence of the British National Party and the Stephen Lawrence killers; it was not quietly and deeply woven into every aspect of society. One of my first encounters of racism was being told by my white best friend at school that I could not attend her First Holy Communion because her dad did not like black people. I remember feeling so hurt that, despite the depth of our friendship, me and my black skin were unwelcome. **>**

DESPITE THE DEPTH OF OUR FRIENDSHIP, ME AND MY

BLACK SKIN WERE UNWELCOME

Sadly, racism is often more subtle. Racism was society deeming me unattractive because my skin was too dark and my nose was too wide. It was the absence of black faces and bodies in my favourite teenage magazines. As I got older, it was the lack of representation in my university teaching staff, my phD programme, and every workplace I have been in.

It is the constant feeling of being alone in predominantly white institutions, despite living in the racially diverse city of London. It is the world's constant reminder of what is yours and what is not.

Racism is exhausting! As a black person living in the UK, society wants to shrink you. It manifests as a colleague telling you that your academic career will be easy because people only care about minorities now. Racism is learning you will never climb high enough to escape its grips. Racism tells you to display the most palatable version of yourself to avoid being labelled an angry black woman. There is a lot to be angry about!

LIFE
WILL SHOW YOU THAT
HARD WORK DOES
NOT
ALWAYS PAY.

Sometimes I think about the phrase, 'Work twice as hard for half as much', and while it may hold more truth than the slogans that I was brought up with, it would have demotivated me. Why work for half? The expressions my parents gave me made me into the ambitious person I am today. It made me strive for more and believe in myself. Now in my thirties, through hard work, resilience, and the support of many amazing people, I am starting to achieve some of the goals set by my younger self. I proudly hold the title 'Doctor', I love my job, and I am no longer poor.

Nonetheless, over time, life will show you that hard work does not always pay. Hard work is not enough because, if it was, why would there be so few black people in powerful positions? As I continue to work to climb the academic career ladder, I notice more and more people that look like me disappearing from these structures. I often wonder, why am I still here? At the moment it is my love of the immune system, my continued need to avoid NFA status, and my goal to be that black Immunology lecturer inspiring the next generation. The enduring worry is always what could halt my goals: a lack of ability or racism? I am never sure. What I do know is that no matter how hard I work, racism will still be there, standing in the doorway, but that does not mean I will not make it through.

Dr Faith Uwadiae.
Immunologist.

Faith works for the Francis Crick Institute. As a woman of colour in science, she is well known for campaigning for black scientists to receive more recognition in their fields.

RACISM IS EXHAUSTING!

Chef Orlando

The first time racism struck home was in my first job in a kitchen. I was born in Birmingham, England, of Caribbean parents, and grew up in a mixed ethnic society. I got my first job in a hotel, where I was the only employee of colour and I was called names by the other employees – the allusions to monkeys and trees were not helped by the fact that I am of short stature. One day the chef slapped me for being cheeky. (I slapped him back.)

The next time I felt I was being treated differently was here in St Lucia, interestingly. Twenty years ago, I took the post of executive chef in one of the most prestigious hotels in the Caribbean. The managerial staff of these resorts are usually white expats, and although I cannot recall any outright example of discrimination, I always had the feeling that I was not quite included and that I had to be twice as good to be tolerated. On the other hand, the locals thought of me as an Englishman and, to an extent, still do after twenty years, and this has its own set of problems.

Chef Orlando.

A leading advocate for Caribbean cuisine, Chef Orlando was born in the UK and relocated to St Lucia, where he is at the helm of the Soufrière restaurant Orlando's. The restaurant prides itself on using locally grown products, and supporting farmers and fishermen from the surrounding communities.

Shereener Browne

ACTRESS, PRODUCER, AND BARRISTER

YOUR
ALL–WHITE
SOCIAL BUBBLES

Untitled #1

Some of you
    Posted a black tile on your socials
    You did this for
#BlackOutTuesday

Some of you
Compiled reading lists
Lists of blogs to listen to
You made purchases from black-owned
businesses For #SupportBlackOwnedDay

Some of you
Made placards emblazoned with the
words: #BlackLivesMatter

You marched
Mouth and nose obscured by masks
In your all-white social bubbles
To your all-white town centres

Some of you
See us as the Noble Savage
To your White Saviour
The victim
To your hero
Some of you
Only have black people in your house
To clean or
To look after your children
Some of you
Smile warmly   **>**

At your children's diverse friendship group
　Whilst secretly praying
　Your daughter never lies down
　With a black man
　Some of you
　Are happy to go for after-work drinks
　With your 'colleague of colour'
　The one you never invite to your home for
the annual family barbecue
　The one who is perpetually
　Overlooked for promotion
　Some of you
　Stiffen, ever so slightly,
　When you see my son,
　Holding your belongings ever tighter as he
passes whilst secretly desiring his body
　Some of you
　Ask my son for drugs

When he is hanging out with friends
You will not take 'no' for an answer
Some of you
Made me an Honorary White
Because I am a barrister
And I am married to someone
You consider part of your tribe
For some of you
I am your token Black Friend
Some. Of. You.

FOR SOME OF YOU
I AM YOUR

Shereener Browne.
Actress, producer, and barrister.

Shereener specializes in all aspects of equality, diversity law, and media law. She won the Sidney Elland Goldsmith Bar Pro Bono Award for her unpaid work in employment and discrimination law. She is the founder of a black-led theatre company called Orison Productions.

TOKEN BLACK FRIEND

·

Allan
Willmot

SECOND WORLD - WAR RAF VETERAN

Now You Know Me

I was born in 1925 and volunteered first for the Royal Navy in 1941, when there was a call for volunteer servicemen from Jamaica. At 16½, I saw an advertisement in the *Jamaica Gleaner* newspaper saying that the British Government needed recruits for the Royal Navy. I applied, passed the test, and was accepted.

My service on the ship HMS *Hauken*, in the Caribbean theatre of war, had its dangers, which came mainly from German submarines in the area. They often sank British and Allied tankers, as well as cargo boats. For instance, on 25 May 1942, the SS *Empire Beatrice*, an unescorted and unarmed cargo ship, was sunk by a torpedo fired by a German U-boat. At the time, I was among the team that rescued nine survivors from a raft and took them to Kingston, Jamaica.

However, I felt my career was not progressing fast enough. At the same time, the British Government began to recruit Jamaican volunteers for the Royal Air Force ground crew, and advertisements were published in the *Jamaica Gleaner* in late 1943. I applied to the

RAF and was accepted. I got along well with my white British colleagues, but less so with white American soldiers, who were openly racist. Fights broke out in pubs and dance halls, and they were always defeated.

After the Second World War ended, the British were quick to demob thousands of West- Indian servicemen and women. I was among them, and having returned to Jamaica in 1946, I felt that it was not the place in which I wanted to settle down, and so I returned to London. Life in London, in the winter of 1947, was not pleasant, but I survived. I often slept in trains at the London Underground train terminus. Racism in those days was overt, 'in your face'. It soon dawned on me that I could employ my talent in London's show business, and I did so with a degree of success with the Southlanders, a male singing quartet that dominated the entertainment scene from the 1950s to the early 1970s. The Southlanders shared the stage with most of Britain's popular performers, including Jimmy Young, Morecambe and Wise, Vera Lynne, the Andrews Sisters, Marty Wilde,

Max Bygraves, Tommy Trinder, Petula Clark, Tommy Cooper, Tony Hancock, Bruce Forsyth, Helen Shapiro, David Frost, Norman Vaughan, Shirley Bassey, Tommy Steele, Cliff Richard and the Shadows, to name but a few. Also, the Southlanders' hit records like 'I am a Mole and I Live in a Hole' were produced at Abbey Road Studios by George Martin, whose productions, in the 1960s, made the Beatles' music a national and international favourite.

After twenty-four years in the business and with stiff competition from such young talented groups, I realized my days as an entertainer were numbered. I obtained a job in the Post Office Telecommunications Department in 1974, and retired from the service in 1990. During the three decades that followed, I have played an important role in the establishment of the West-Indian Ex-Services Association (now the West-Indian Association of Service Personnel).

In the 1980s they obtained a permanent meeting place at 161, Clapham Manor Street, south London. The aim was to ensure that their contributions and service would not be forgotten by the present and future generations of British people. Their members provide social services voluntarily.

I have held various positions of responsibility in the association over the years, including President. From 1998, I have been a member of the Memorial Gate Council, which is chaired by Baroness Flather. The Memorial Gates, a war memorial, located at the Hyde Park Corner end of Constitution Hill in London, commemorates the armed forces of the British Empire from Africa, the Caribbean, and the five regions of the Indian subcontinent, including Bangladesh, India, Nepal, Pakistan, and Sri Lanka who served in both world wars. The memorial was officially inaugurated in 2002 by Her Majesty the Queen.

I published my memoirs in 2015, entitled *Now You Know*, and believe that they will help others to read about the contribution I and others have made to Britain from 1941 to the present day.

Allan Wilmot.
Second World War RAF veteran.

Allan continues to serve communities in the UK, and on 16 April 2019 he received the Certificate of Recognition from the Mayor of Lambeth, for his voluntary work in the borough.

Kayisha Payne

SCIENTIST

Facts Not Feelings

There is a bitter thread running through an industry where

Life is the highest cost, the alchemist's dream, and where

It is manufactured on the sweat of bodies withheld from

The ease and sympathy it can have. A storm rides under

This shadowed underbelly, blooming across petri dishes,

Under careful observation of microscopes, noted only by

The least privileged eyes in the room. No screening

Or testing can pull it through like bones from a fish,

Loose stitch, and no pale hands would think to drag through

That mire of miscalculation, lack of concern.

That bitterness chokes through in the statistics that you

Like to ignore. Where is peer review when the toll rises

Higher on a sea of society's least cared for?

I don the white coat, speak in numbers that seem to

Ring truer to surprised ears than the blood on knees

Of authority across another sea's country. But that

'That bitterness chokes through in the statistics that you like to ignore'

Is just it. The numbers stay silent now that life has

Been stripped by someone who should know the power

Of figures and figureheads. Now the facts can be ignored

As an act of sympathy – they see the one man, and so

Every heaving mind stacking the odds for the safety of

All creeds can be understood. Now they see me, now

I am spotlit under an infinite gamma-ray gaze, and they care

About the facts I can spout. But it is so easy to smear

Gold over numbers and call it progress, rather than see

The blood and sweat beneath it, and redistribute the load.

Kayisha Payne.
Scientist.

Kayisha has a master's degree in Chemical Engineering, with a focus on Biochemistry. She is the founder of the non-profit organization BBSTEM, has been recognized as one of the top 100 most influential leaders in diversity and technology, and was a recipient of the STEM Rising Star Award at the Black British Business Awards.

Ray
Emmet Brown

ACTOR,
WRITER,
FATHER,
AND LEGAL
DEFENCE

I remember when I was a solicitor's clerk and used to sit behind counsel in court taking notes. On one particular occasion we had a case at the Old Bailey. I'd worked all over London but had never worked at the Bailey. So, knowing how iconic it was, I made a special effort to dress the part. Suited, booted, with briefcase in hand, I walked into court, following the barrister we had instructed. No sooner had I stepped into the court than the court clerk quickly came from the front of the court and opened the dock door indicating for me to go in. I kindly informed her I was part of the defendant's legal team. She apologized profusely and I took my seat behind counsel.

On another occasion at Southwark Crown Court, I was again acting as a solicitor's clerk, in a suit, sitting behind counsel, as the lead detective in the case gave his evidence in the witness box. All through his evidence he kept staring at me, which I found a bit strange. After he had given his evidence the court was adjourned for a tea break and I went to have a cuppa just outside the court. The detective who had just given evidence bowled over to me stating that he knew me from somewhere. He asked me was I on his patch? I shook my head. He then asked me was I known to the police? – a euphemism for did I have a criminal record. I again shook my head. He then asked had he arrested me, or had I had any dealings with police? I shook my head and said 'no' to all of his questions. He then changed his tone and asked if he knew me socially. I said I didn't think so. At this point I could have told him that I was also an actor and that most coppers recognized me from *Life on Mars*, or from one of the many other TV shows I had done like *Prime Suspect*, but because of his opening gambit and insistence that I had been in trouble with the law, I thought it best just to let him stew.

The point of these two stories – and they are by no means the worst incidents I've faced – is that in both cases, no matter how smart I looked, it didn't matter, as all they saw first was the colour of my skin, which in their eyes meant something negative. Now, imagine if you were a young black guy, not dressed in suit, driving in your car, walking home, or riding a bike, being stopped repeatedly by the police, not because you'd done anything wrong, but because of the colour your skin . . . How angry would you be?

Ray Emmet Brown.
Actor, writer, father, and legal defence.
Ray is a winner of The *Manchester Evening News* Theatre Award for Best Actor in a Supporting Role, and a nominee for Best Actor in the Screen Nation Awards.

Diana Dahlia

BUSINESSWOMAN

I am one of the Creative Directors of Diana Dahlia PR (DDPR). I made the decision to start my own public relations company after several years of working for global corporations. This whole journey started some thirty years ago, when I literally stumbled into the world of media, fashion, beauty, TV, radio, journalism, luxury lifestyle, and events, and this has been my personal world ever since. But it has not always been like this.

Racism, racial and gender discrimination affected me professionally and personally in the workplace, including barriers to promotion, the stereotyped belief that we black people are incompetent, a lack of mentorship, and feelings of isolation. I would often choose to focus on the aspects that I was able to control, such as my social skills, dress, and speech, and remained optimistic about my circumstances.

I didn't allow my sense of value to come from other people. I made a conscious decision to not live for society. I live for myself. This resulted in me wearing my naturally curly hair instead of it being blow-ried straight; dressing to my own standards, and paving my own way.

It was important to follow my goals motivate myself, as I was alone with no support. I did not feel obligated to act or look a certain way just to fit in.

You have to know who you are first. think wearing my natural hair in the work environment helped me with that process – not being ashamed of my hair, or my individual style, or name. Instead, using that as a point of conversation with other people – for example, when they asked, 'Why does your hair look like that?' – I used it as an opportunity to explain. I said that there are well-educated people who don't have to dress in a suit and tie, or wear their hair a certain way. There are educated people in all facets of life, and I learnt very early that racism affects black people no matter your status.

Unfortunately, to minimize stress and to cope with racism and sexism, I would work longer hours, or go over and beyond what is typically required. Whereas some saw this as an effective strategy, others noted that this approach generated more stress for me, which I have to agree was true. I responded by focusing on my own definitions of black womanhood through self-valuation, the freedom to be one's self and not seek validation from others. This specifically embraces self-definition and that assists black women in seeing the circumstances shaping race, class, and gender oppression. To keep sane, I acknowledged that racial oppression, strong black woman syndrome, and social injustice would always be part of my life, and that vision, dignity, and self-worth wouldn't succeed if I didn't stay positive.

Is there such a thing as the perfect balance? If someone tells you there is, they are being economical with the truth. You can only strive for harmony as defined by you at any given point in time. The key is to do what you love and only do it because you want to do it. Your friends and family will understand you are doing what feeds your passion. Parallel to that you always also have to remember that, at the end of the day, the company you keep close is one of the most important things in the world.

I believe the love you share, feel, and receive is truly what makes the world a better place. You can't be great at everything, and you can't be everywhere all the time. So choose, and live with your choices. Do what feeds your soul, and do all you can to be the best version of yourself for you and those around you.

My motto is you should always be the best you can be. A strong, independent woman has the courage to be the best version of herself. Sometimes it just takes a little reminder that helps us to realize the incredible potential

that lies within us. As a woman, you not only provide the necessary essentials for life, but you also have the power to create life. You are able to transform and to change, which allows you to leave all negativity behind. Don't allow others to make decisions about your life, but instead regain your power, be self-motivated, and seize the power that lies within you.

Diana Dahlia.
Businesswoman.

Diana is the founder and creative director of Diana Dahlia PR. She is renowned as a fashion brand specialist, top fashion model, and former actress. For several years she earned major endorsements from various global brands.

Albert
Amankona

FINANCIAL ANALYST,
POLITICAL COMMENTATOR,
AND ACTIVIST

From when we are children, we can tell what is good and bad, right and wrong, from what our friends, family, teachers, and other people tell us. But no one told me that 'white was good' and 'black was bad', so how does a child figure that out? Its foundations may come from structural racism, fallout from Europe's colonial past and the racial hierarchy Empire left. Also, a dysfunctional father-son relationship: my father was largely absent during my childhood; when he was around, he was imperious with his belief of what it meant to be black, revealed by his 'African' parental style, calling me 'Akim' instead of 'Albie', insisting what food I should and shouldn't eat, how he wanted my hair to be cut, and things he wanted me to have an interest in. He seemed disappointed that I took more of an interest in my English heritage over my Ghanaian heritage, that I preferred my mother to him – 'white' over 'black'. Blackness felt forced upon me as a child, so I rejected it.

'WHY DO YOU SPEAK LIKE THAT?' 'OREO', 'HALFIE'

But it's more than that. Strangely, looking back, it's been reaffirmed much of the time by how I have been treated by fellow black people. At secondary school, other black students often made comments like, 'Why do you speak like that?' 'You speak like a white person'; 'Coconut', 'Oreo', 'Halfie', and 'Batty Boy'. My friends were people I knew from primary school: we all spoke the same because we all came from the same primary school; we were all academic; for whatever reason, we all spoke the same – in a 'white' way. I was bullied so badly at my first school that I left. Not only did I not want to be around my school bullies, I didn't want to be anything like them. At my second school I was inadvertently one of four black students in my year. It also happened to be one of the best schools in London. The bullying stopped.

University was more diverse with how people looked, but less so with regard to background. **>**

I learnt about black history and discovered my sexuality. I was introduced to colonialism/postcolonialism, patriarchy, gender theory, Kinsey's Scale, unconscious bias, among other things. I elected to take modules on 'black' courses: Fanon, Césaire, and Du Bois taught me about blackness in a way my father could not. I was also introduced to other ideas, which I questioned and rejected: no-platforming, cancel culture, cultural appropriation, anti-capitalism, and anti-free speech. Those who didn't roll their eyes and laugh when I asked those questions and advocated free speech, free minds, and free markets tended to be white. It felt similar to being back at school, but I could speak for myself, knew I was a good debater, and there was no threat of violence, so there was an element of relishing the disagreements I got into.

Entering employment at a City financial services firm, I found myself one of four black people in a client-facing, revenue-generating role in the London office. Most of our support staff were black, one with a first-class Law degree from Bristol University. All of the cleaners were black. And, we've wound up in a similar place as we have done in every paragraph of this entry: white good; black bad. Many of the reasons why we keep returning to this are out of our control. Racism and its causes can't be dismantled unilaterally, but as black people we can do more with what we do control: chiefly, how we treat one and other and what we define as 'black' vs. 'white'.

My education, work, and life experiences have allowed me to understand blackness, and the reasons why people are racist in the broader context of history, philosophy, economics, and policy decisions – thus, the homophobia I had faced from black students at school; the reasons why I was terrified to come out to my African family and not my English family; and why one of my only black friends at work was a top Bristol Law graduate who worked in a support role.

However, it has also taught me that there is not one way to be black. Not one way to think, to vote, to dress, to listen to music, love, speak, or behave. We speak often about the limits that society imposes on us as a result of racism, but little about the limits we put on ourselves by defining whether or not something is 'black'.

There is not a black or white way to speak; who we love is not black or white; our lives are not black and white; so good and bad are not black and white. As black people, we should empower each other to go forth and paint the world black in whichever area we please, not decide which parts are black and which parts aren't. Racism is real, but we don't need to oppress each other into our individual ideas of what black is on top of everything else.

We are all black, beautiful, and brave. Let's remember to always strive to see that in each other, especially when we may disagree, when we live in a society which does not always see it in us.

Albert Amankona.
Financial analyst, political commentator, and activist.

Albert is the cofounder of CARFE, the UK's first centre-right organization for improving race relations.

WE ARE ALL BLACK, BEAUTIFUL, AND BRAVE. LET'S REMEMBER TO ALWAYS STRIVE TO SEE THAT IN EACH OTHER

Kaya Lockiby -Belgrave

FORENSIC PSYCHOLOGIST IN TRAINING

We experience the most growth when we operate from a place of pain.

So when, as a society, will we grow? Or is pain only limited? Does our empathy for those in pain only extend as far as those who look like us?

'Come on, let us black girls line up at the front.'

As she declared this, my best friend grabbed my hand and I tottered with her to the front of the line. One of the girls we walked past pointed at me and said, 'But she's not black! She's white!' My friend turned around to her and said, 'Don't be silly. Of course she's black!' That interaction was the first time I realized that I was different. I was 5.

I recognize I was fortunate to not experience overt racism. 'Fortunate' feels like a very strange word to use. What makes subtle racism so insidious is that it sows the seed of doubt in your mind. Was that really racist? Maybe I am just being sensitive? That is what we need to watch out for. **>**

No, you are not being sensitive, and yes, it was racist. I watched a debate about racism on YouTube. I made the mistake of reading through the comments. The overall gist was that, as black people, we have no right to feel our pain because everyone has suffered. Imagine telling someone that you are hurting only to be given ten reasons why their hurt is more significant than yours.

Here are a few of my experiences.

'You're not like other black girls.'

'You don't sound black.'

'But you're not really black, are you. You must be mixed with something!'

'So, which one of your parents is white?'

'Oh, are you the young lady I spoke to on the phone? You speak so well.'

'Why don't you wear your hair in an Afro?'

'Black b****!'

It's laughable, as if black has a sound. As if you've met every single black girl in the world, making your statement all the more accurate. As if black people come in one shade. As if it makes a difference to your life knowing whether I have a white parent. As if my complexion didn't match my voice. As if my hair is to be worn for your personal pleasure. As if I am a black female dog. As if . . . I am not human and I do not have feelings. Yet when I raise my concerns, they are downplayed: 'We are all mixed really.' Or worse, I am pitied for what I cannot change, and pitied due to the ignorance of others.

Growing up, I believed that the sky was the limit. I was reaching for the sky when the glass ceiling blocked my ascent. At 14, I learnt that the glass ceiling was my limit. When I was younger, I had hopes of becoming an actress. I attended a small drama school based in north London and signed up for their agency. I waited by my phone with bated breath, hoping for it to ring with offers to attend auditions. It did not ring. A friend of mine was also having a similar experience, so she had the great idea to ask our agent why we were not being booked for jobs. Our agent took one look at us and said, 'If I got a call for an English family, I couldn't exactly put you two forward.' There it was: I was not English because I was not white. Despite being born here, despite my father being born here, I was not English. What I heard was, 'You could never be English. And you would never be good enough to succeed in a market where the demand for white skin is high.'

I gave up on my dream of being an actress, mainly because I didn't think I could make it. I instead pursued my second dream of becoming a forensic psychologist. After six years of applying for posts and attending countless interviews up and down the country, I was given a role as a Forensic Psychologist in Training, working in a prison in Suffolk. I remember that jaws practically dropped when people saw me. One person even said, 'It's nice seeing someone like you in the position that you are in.' I smiled. It looks like I have chosen the right dream. This is the dream that I am going to smash that glass ceiling with. Watch me. See me. I am here.

K

Kaya Lockiby-Belgrave.
Forensic Psychologist in Training.
Kaya works for the Prison Service. A former actor, she loves reading, writing, cats, and dancing. Her aim in life is to spread joy and kindness. Kaya says, 'I believe that I am magic, because I am.'

I REMEMBER THAT JAWS PRACTICALLY DROPPED WHEN PEOPLE SAW ME

Brendon Winter

COMMUNITY POLICE OFFICER

I was born in Chiswick and grew up in Hanwell, Ealing. I am the eldest of four brothers and a proud father of a son and a daughter. Mum was from Grenada, Dad is Antiguan, and my stepmum is Jamaican.

My parents came to England in the 1960s as children, and the racism they suffered was far worse than what I have had to face. Mum said white people used to say that our skin was dirty and we didn't wash ourselves. Back then, my dad and uncles would deal with racist kids with their fists, even at school.

I am a community support worker, love my job bringing communities together and giving advice to the youth of today. In an ideal world we want equality, but we will continue the fight for it.

Black people are always treated differently from white people by the police. I am not saying that all police officers are the same. I have never been subjected to police brutality and I have met more good officers than bad ones, growing up in Ealing, but I have often been stopped for no good reason.

Once I was stopped on my way home at around 3 a.m. by two police officers. They asked me where I was going, and I said 'home'. They then asked me where I lived and I said 'right here', as I was actually outside my house. They didn't believe me, and they gave me a look. I got my keys out and opened the first door, and they were still there. They watched me open the second door before they walked on.

When I was growing up my parents always said one thing you should never do when stopped by the Law is to retaliate. They taught me to be polite and compliant. If not, I was playing into their hands. I was also told to get the name or names of the officers that stopped me if I was treated unfairly. That's what I did the many times I was stopped in the 1990s when I was growing up.

At the time my family and I were living on the Medway Estate in Perivale, where 70 per cent of the people who lived there were white, and I think the police acted funny when they saw non-whites living in an affluent area.

I WORRY
ABOUT THE FUTURE
FOR OUR YOUNG GENERATION

I have told my kids the same thing that my parents taught me. I tell them to always obey the law. My son has been stopped a few times by police, and I believe the only reason he has never been in cuffs is because he is always polite to the officers.

I was not happy when he was searched on the ground. He filmed the incident as he was also unhappy with the search. As my son was being searched, he said to them, 'My dad does what you do.' They didn't believe him. They let him go, but I have told him that if it happens again he should take their names and shoulder numbers.

He didn't have a problem with being stopped; he just didn't like their approach, or their attitude towards him. This happened in Southall, an area where there are Asian people, and I know they face more issues with the police there than black people do.

Mum always told us that as adults we would have to work twice as hard as a white person. That's why Black Lives Matter is such a very important movement for people of all colours. I feel this is a movement that has brought people of all colours together around the world to try to change this.

I still feel very bitter about what has happened to black people over the years and the recent police brutality. George Floyd's murder sickened me, as did the deaths of Breonna Taylor, Rayshard Brooks, Atatiana Jefferson, and many more that I could name.

My kids don't hang out in the street with their friends, and are very sensible, but I do worry about them when they are out there. I worry about the future for our young generation. Still, it's easier for them than it was for my parents, or even me. We just have to take it day by day.

Brendon Winter.
Community police officer.
Brendon has many years of experience in his job and believes in bringing people together.

Jackee Holder

EXECUTIVE AND LEADERSHIP COACH,
AUTHOR AND INTERFAITH MINISTER

Some of the happiest times back in the 1960s were when family friends from Ealing, in west London, would come to visit at bank holidays, bringing their children with them. We would request to go to the park knowing that because our parents were happy to see their friends, the answer would be a definite 'yes'. There must have been at least eight of us walking and laughing as we headed up to Tivoli Park, a small park located at the top of Knight's Hill, in south-east London. Our ultimate goal was to get to the swings and the roundabout, and play to our heart's content.

Some of my cousins were older than me and I felt really safe. The park was a public space, or so at least we thought. Within a few minutes of arriving, we became aware of a group of older white children approaching us. When the first stone hit, it got our attention almost in the same moment. Then another just missed one of my brothers and without saying a word to each other we all started running for the main gates. Even though we exchanged no words between us, our collective minds knew what to do – head for the main gates and don't look back. That memory of the hushed silence as we

fled across the park lawns being chased by a group of children whose skin colour was the opposite of ours was my first real encounter with racism based on the colour of my skin.

We made it safely home that afternoon. I don't remember us hugging each other, or really talking about what had happened. I just recall an unspoken knowing each child felt in their bones: to escape, to flee, was instinctual. Memories live in our bodies. Memories of ancestors being hunted through sugar canes and woods. The scene could have been a repeated memory of the past in the present. We knew without being told that we were seen as a threat. That there are places we were not welcome, and that we always have to be vigilant, on guard for attack.

I'd like to tell you that things have gotten better fifty and more years later, but I simply would be lying. Only last year I was sitting in my car in Crystal Palace on the main road. I was relieved as I had found a good place to park, to go and enjoy a spot of lunch. I saw the car in front of me blocking the traffic with its left indicator light on. After a few minutes it occurred to me that they might be thinking I was leaving when

I had only just arrived. Before I could even wind down my window to indicate that I wasn't leaving a woman flew out of the car and hurled a torrent of abuse into the air directly towards me. At first, I thought it was a joke, but I realized that her anger was actually directed towards me when I heard words like 'nigger' and 'black bitch'. I stepped out of my car and indicated to her to bring her sorry-arse self onto the pavement, where I intended to confront her. I turned around just in time to see the woman charging towards me at full speed, like a bull in a ring, shimmering with rage. In that spilt second, I rooted myself to the spot, unlike the 8-year-old back in 1969 whose survival instinct was to take flight and run. Instead, my nearly 60-year-old self held the ground Samurai-warrior style. I became a woman not for turning. She stopped a hair's breadth away, screaming abuse into my face while her boyfriend stood back, holding their small dog, surveying the scene with a wry look on his face. I knew in that moment that if I moved, or flexed a muscle and responded physically I probably, would not be here to tell the tale.

Jackee Holder.
Executive and leadership coach, author and interfaith minister.

Jackee is the author of *Soul Purpose: Be Your Own Best Life Coach* and *49 Ways to Write Yourself Well*. Her work, as a conference host, workshop facilitator, and personal development coach, has taken her across the globe.

Andrea E. L. Attipoe

BIOENGINEERING PhD STUDENT

'Why Me?'

I remember the sound the spray can made as it struck my face. I remember the smell of the paint as he sprayed my face, the coldness of the individual colourful drops mixing with the heat, and the pain on my black skin. I remember the second of confusion, which didn't really feel like a second, but rather like an untimely event, something out of this era and my modern reality.

Is this what a police officer is supposed to do? Is this really happening to me? Why is this happening to me? Why me?

Why me?

As I was handcuffed and thrown in a police van, I remember asking just that and being told that the officer, 'Could have put his 9mm on my forehead.' I don't think words can convey how terrifying a statement like that is to a beaten 17-year-old boy, from a man whose black, shining firearm is a gesture of the hand away. I suppose his colleague perceived that fear and secretly told me, in a failed attempt to comfort, 'I don't know why he did that. It will be okay.

Just be quiet.' Quiet? Quiet when your whole entire being is screaming within itself? I remember the humiliation and the shame, I remember the blame, I remember feeling guilty. Why do *I* feel guilty?

Why me?

I spent the next four hours locked in a cage. More potently, I felt trapped inside my own mind. I remember the stream of thoughts that flooded my head, and within all that turbulence a single question seemed to persistently emerge from the deep:

Why me?

The key that unlocked that prison cell did not release the shackles which continued to restrain my mind. I gave them my address so that they could drive me home and they scoffed in disbelief. At the time, I remember thinking, *Why would I lie about my own address?* So many questions and too few answers I could provide to myself, as I was getting ready to try and explain to my parents what had just happened to me. As the door opened, my mother wept, but what I did not expect is how calm my father was. As the police officers pronounced words I cannot even remember, he was staring at me quietly. He asked: 'What happened to you? Why is your face like that?' as if the two uniformed figures standing in our living room didn't even exist. 'They did this to me.'

Within his look I saw a fury rise; the same fire that had been burning me up inside, the same heat I had seen in his eyes every time a police officer stopped him beyond any reason in the streets of Brussels. The officers called their superior, who said, 'There was clearly a mistake. We did not expect a family like yours in a residential neighbourhood like this. When I turned into your alley and saw the car outside, I understood we did not understand who we were dealing with.'

That was the answer to my recurring question. My colour determined the way in which I was treated, and no amount of spray paint on my skin could change what they saw underneath. In the same way that no number of complaints and court procedures ever brought my father and me the justice I deserved. I even think the internal report said that I had hit and sprayed my own face in the police van, with my hands cuffed behind my back. Unsurprising to a 17-year-old boy whose faith in a system and its enforcers was shattered to pieces. The events of that night never left me. I am still afraid of the police today, always asking myself if I am doing anything wrong every time their sirens screech, always under the threat of the unsanctioned and remorseless violence they exerted on me. My mind remains eternally trapped in the cage they locked me in.

I kept the voucher for the party I didn't attend that night, as if that unripped ticket could one day buy me a trip out of this fear.

Andrea E. L. Attipoe.
Bioengineering Ph.D. student.

Having spent most of his life in Belgium, Andrea is studying at Imperial College London, and is particularly interested in insect adhesion. One day he hopes to help create bio-inspired adhesives which will replicate the performance of their biological originals.

Sonia Campbell

COMPANY SECRETARY

From Windrush to the Home Office

A Windrush child who migrated from Jamaica to London, I had never met a white person until I boarded the plane with my two brothers in 1967. I had no concept of blackness until primary school. It was a severe culture shock when I had to deal with hostile white children. I was bullied for my natural plaited hair and Jamaican accent. I quickly learnt to speak formal English by reading everything, I loved reading. I was a shy, introverted girl and their hostility also made me a solitary thinker.

My school days were characterized by aggressive white teachers, who used corporal punishment for my trivial mistakes. They also had low expectations of me. At 16, despite excellent exam results, the careers officer told me to get a job at Woolworths. But my father said, 'My daughter wants to study law and I support her ambitions.'

My mother also told me, 'Make sure that

you get something in your head before you get married and have children.'

My A levels results got me into a polytechnic. I was focused and achieved an upper second-class Sociology degree. I felt blessed not to have the many obstacles faced by other black female students who, without financial support from their parents, had to leave the course early. But my academic success came at a personal cost. In order to fit in, I abandoned my Jamaican roots and accent, as white lecturers and students thought they were comical.

By 1980 my plan to escape from home and gain my independence was under way. After 150 rejection letters, I accepted a role as a retail management trainee with Sainsbury's supermarkets, and got the wake-up call that a single degree did not open doors for black women. I was ridiculed for being too formal and for bringing a briefcase to work. My personality also came under attack when I was told I would never become a branch personnel officer because of it. So, I learnt to work smarter and to be more flexible professionally. I bowed to peer pressure, permed my natural hair, and began wearing make-up to fit into white office culture.

I left Sainsbury's for a junior public-sector role in employee relations, the only black woman in the team, and started the Chartered Institute of Personnel and Development (CIPD) course at evening classes. By this time I had learnt how to communicate with my older white colleagues and to gain their respect.

I entered senior management taking on challenging roles, developing policies, and managing budgets and teams. I had my two children, completed my master's degree, and achieved Fellow status with the CIPD.

I am proud that I am a positive role model for my daughters

Yet despite my qualifications, hard work, and achievements, there were still barriers to my progression. After my divorce, I moved cities in 2000, to my most senior role in Birmingham City Council's HR team. The role was professionally challenging, but despite being good at it, I wasn't promoted, because I was not 'visible' to the controlling Labour councillors. In reality, the HR team was dominated by white men, and being a single parent proved a major obstacle to success.

I then did three Civil Service jobs in the Department for Education and the Home Office, where I faced racism and sexism from managers and HR staff, who could barely disguise how much they hated having a black female HR manager.

I became a lay member of the Employment Tribunal. A powerful and influential role. Many claimants were female, black, and had no legal representation. I was able to make a difference for these women by helping to ensure they had a fair hearing.

Already fatigued with fighting sexism and racism, I was now also facing age discrimination. So, I took voluntary redundancy and started my own limited company.

My eldest daughter has graduated and now works for the NHS. Some things are easier for her than they were for me, but she still has some struggles as an ambitious black woman.

I know now that my personal life and wellbeing are more important than any job, and I am proud that I am a positive role model for my daughters and other young women.

Sonia Campbell.
Company secretary.

Sonia is the mother of two grown-up daughters. She is a Fellow of the Chartered Institute of Personal Development, with thirty-eight years' experience in people development. Sonia is a lay member of the Employment Tribunal.

Kevin Maxwell

WRITER AND FORMER DETECTIVE

I DID NOT REALIZE HOW BAD RACISM WAS WITHIN THE POLICE FORCE

Playing My Part

Until writing my book *Forced Out*, about my time in the British police as a black gay officer and reflecting on my life, I did not realize how bad racism was within the police force and society generally.

Growing up in an interracial, close-knit, working-class community in Liverpool, as a mixed-race boy born to a white mother and black father, I did not think about the impact of racism on me and others like me. That was despite having negative interactions with officers who saw my colour first and humanity second: like being outside my home as a teenager on my bike and asked to account for my presence; or with my mother walking home one night with officers pulling alongside us, and asking her if she was okay – because a young brown boy, with a much older white woman, his mum, somehow gave them cause for concern.   **>**

I never thought about the impact of these interactions until adulthood. One of the reasons for that was my mum. She had encouraged me to have a heart as open and generous as hers, not succumbing to suspicion, fear, or hate. More so, when leaving my secondary school, Stephen Lawrence, a black teenager like myself in London, was brutally murdered by a gang of white men, with the police failing him and his family. The force was later labelled 'institutionally racist'.

It would have been easy for me to hate the police, like many other men of colour, because of their lived experience and interactions with officers, but I did not want to be like that. I joined Greater Manchester Police and later transferred to London's Metropolitan Police. Racism blighted my career. I now understand what so many black and brown people have been saying all these years.

Twenty years after Stephen's death, and forty years after riots broke out in my neighbourhood, Toxteth, in Liverpool, owing to the mistreatment of people of colour by the police, things are worse now than ever. Statistics show the disproportionate targeting of black and brown communities with controversial police powers such as stop and search, as well as tasering and arrests. These have unfairly impacted minority ethnic communities, and done nothing to address youth violence. Young people feel alienated as a result.

In Britain, we consider America to have a terrible record for racism in the police, without acknowledging what is going on at home. Brutality, racism, and the denial of civil liberties in the UK simply don't receive the same sort of scrutiny. Racism and discrimination are a cultural issue in our police. The force is systemically racist towards non-white people. Until we admit it, these things are never going to change. The idea that racism is down to a few bad apples is long gone.

Black officers and staff have spoken over many years of their experiences of racism in Britain's police. It has broken many physically and mentally. The spirit of good officers destroyed. In my case, the police were found guilty of discriminating, harassing, and victimizing me over forty times because of the colour of my skin. So how far have we come? How much has changed?

Many people do not understand the extent of racism in the police and its surrounding culture, which impacts the very communities it is sworn to protect. The police do not know how to deal with race issues or racism. They cannot change from within, however much they think they can. The leadership's strategy to improve policing has always been safe and never implemented with urgency or compulsion – the public, press, and politicians have to enforce the change.

To engage with changing times, we need a police force that actively listens and accepts criticism, even when this means losing face and admitting it is in the wrong. A force that does more good than bad, and actively embraces diversity and difference. This involves the police examining hard truths, which they've struggled to do for the past forty years, and is why the same problems persist.

And more black and brown faces are not going to stamp out the racism. We need officers who think differently and don't just look different. Though I am not responsible for racism, I live in hope that if I play my part in ending it, we will all live in a more fair, equal, and just society.

Kevin Maxwell.
Writer and former detective.

Kevin's experience as a police officer includes working for both the Greater Manchester Police and the London Metropolitan Police. His book, *Forced Out*, about his time in the police force, is published by Granta. He describes himself as a 'cultural Catholic'.

THE POLICE DO NOT KNOW HOW TO DEAL WITH RACE ISSUES OR RACISM

Professor Uzo Iwobi OBE

LAW PROFESSOR

Let the Rain Fall

In the early 1990s I arrived at London Heathrow to join my husband Dr Andrew Iwobi, Law Lecturer at Swansea University, having had a traumatic and damaging experience of racism in Nigeria, at the hands of the entry clearance officer (ECO) at the British High Commission in Lagos, Nigeria.

It all happened because I was required to process my settlement visa, to enable me to join my husband (who had a right of abode in the UK) and start our newly married lives together. The ECO who interviewed me was not convinced my marriage was real. He accused me of lying and that ours was a fake marriage, as many of my 'kind' faked marriages and faked documents. The abuse, humiliation, and disrespect I'd endured was unacceptable, and finally, the Swansea MP intervened and my visa was granted. We were kept apart for one and half years, as newlyweds fighting to get the visa.

When I arrived in Wales, I settled in Swansea and, in the same week, I went to the Job Centre to ask for help and advice to enable me get a job in the legal profession.

I was told straight up that I could never get a job in the legal profession because I am black! I was absolutely shocked, bewildered, astounded, and I remember saying 'Pardon me?' The lady replied and repeated the same statement and said, 'If you don't believe me, walk from No. 1 to No. 100 of Walter Road in Swansea, where all the solicitors have their offices and try your luck'.

She also advised me very strongly not to use my Ibo name, Uzo, but to choose an English name, which employers could pronounce. And so, although I was no longer a Catholic, I had to change my name from Uzo to 'Linda' Iwobi.

I was determined to prove her wrong.

I wrote so many letters of introduction to law firms and hand-delivered them, and only after delivering over 55 letters did I receive one interview with a firm of solicitors in Swansea's St James Gardens. After a gruelling hour and 30 minutes of interviewing, the owner of the firm (a Welsh man) said to me, 'You are a very intelligent and impressive lady.' I said, 'Thank you. So, does that mean I get the job?' He said, 'Oh no. I just wanted to hear what they teach you in those countries' (referring to whichever country I had come from in Africa). This interview crushed my spirit and as I left that firm, I felt as though the world would collapse around me. There was no ray of hope.

After a few weeks of waiting, I returned to that Job Centre and met the same woman and asked for her advice on the options available to me. She asked me to forget about being a barrister or solicitor because no one cared about that, and just to apply to work in shops such as Sainsbury's, Tesco, Argos, and so on. My first job in the UK was selling toys in Toys "R" Us. I was paid £2.40 per hour. And then I got a nightshift job at Walkers Crisp Factory for £3.60 per hour. I was racially abused in both organizations. I was called a 'black bitch' by customers in Toys "R" Us; another refused to pay at my checkout counter because of my skin colour,

and he made it very clear. At the factory, I found that another African girl who worked there was most often assigned to clean the greasy vats with me on most night shifts. I asked the factory manager whether I was assigned vat duty because I was a black person. They accused me of making trouble, but moved me to other jobs.

When I got a lecturing job a good while later, I was treated less favourably than my white counterparts; I was passed over for promotion numerous times and called names by my colleagues. I took matters to court on two occasions and settled out of court in both cases, with apology letters. My home has been smashed up a number of times by racist young people chanting racist slurs. By God's grace and my tenacity, I was appointed as a Commissioner to the Commission for Racial Equality UK, and I serve as the first black woman Specialist Adviser on Equalities to the Welsh Government. So let the rain fall. We shall not be deterred,

Professor Uzo Iwobi OBE.
Law professor.

Founder of Race Council Cymru, and Specialist Advisor on Equality to the Welsh Government. Nigerian born, Professor Iwobi is dedicated to promoting race equality, art, heritage, and cultural activities for black and minority-ethnic communities across Wales. In 2020, her image was illuminated at the world-famous Stonehenge to commemorate Welsh 'unsung heritage champions', for her work on delivering the first-ever Black History Wales 365 initiative.

Bernadette Thompson

HR PROFESSIONAL AND CIVIL SERVANT

Breathe, breathe and blow. They tell you to do that when you are giving birth to a child
But as a black woman in Britain, I often need to do this to remain calm and to thrive
In a society where it seems so often to be
That distressing things happen to people like me
An incident I just will never forget

On maternity leave so I thought I would get
A bag and some frocks, pair of shoes and some bling
To return to the workplace I needed new things
So, pushing the buggy with a smile on my face,
I entered this shop at a very slow pace
With time on my hands I browsed round the store
But every corner I turned the shop assistant just wore
A hole in the ground, following me round and round
In annoyance I left tutting 'My gosh such a clown'
But this shopping trip turned to a mare
Cos this poor black woman received such a scare
When two shop detectives stopped me in my tracks
And asked if I would open my baby's backpack
Accused of shoplifting! 'You what?' muttered me

THIS BLACK WOMAN

Yes, madam, your backpack we were told, don't you see
  At this point I got it, because I am black,
  Ridiculous but I decided I wouldn't fight back
  The beetroot-faced men became redder until . . .
  I said, 'I am waiting, sirs, for what you said I nicked.' Looking still
  Sheepishly they saw there was nothing to see
  But the stereotype of the black woman – yes, me
  Baby back in the buggy, with my head held high
  I walked back to the shop to stare the assistant in the eye
  You dared to stereotype me for just browsing by

Hmm, well just remember this face next time I come by
  Now the bittersweet end to this tale about me
  This black woman settled out of court with this shop with much glee

Bernadette Thompson.
HR professional and civil servant.
  Bernadette is a notable diversity campaigner, working with leaders across Government to drive a culture of inclusion in the Civil Service. She has held a range of roles within the Civil Service, across many Government departments, including the Ministry of Justice, the Home Office, the Treasury, and the Cabinet Office.

– YES, ME

Dr Sarah
Essilfie-Quaye

PROJECT MANAGER IN
RESEARCH STRATEGY,
IMPERIAL COLLEGE,
LONDON

The impact of racism on my life starts before me. My parents came from Ghana to the Motherland, where the streets are paved with gold! They trained as nurses. When they tried to rent accommodation, they got told, 'No blacks, no dogs, no Irish.'

From Sheffield they moved to Kingston-upon-Hull. This is where I was born. My north London accent hides the fact I'm really a northerner! I have great memories of my early years in 'Ull, but there are also memories of *misunderstandings* that started when I was very young. For example, 'Make-up doesn't work on you. Go over there by

MY PARENTS CAME FROM

GHANA

TO THE

MOTHERLAND

WHERE THE STREETS ARE PAVED WITH GOLD!

yourself and use the chalk' – that was my teacher when I was around 4 years old before a nativity play. I found the statement confusing, as I watched my mum apply her blue eye shadow and pink blush daily (it was the 1980s). But I was too young to argue, and my upbringing had taught me to listen to my teachers. I didn't use the chalk, but I also had (have) a real love-hate relationship with make-up that didn't come from home. I also remember getting a brick through the window and my brother changing schools because of 'bad' treatment. When I was older I understood the reason for these events was racism and that there was much more that had, thankfully, passed over my head.   >

We moved to London a year or so later. At primary school my siblings and I were one of the two black families at the school. I had to deal with frequent racist abuse from many of the other children and was regularly called the N word, the P word (wrong continent, I know), and a G word (think jam jars). My family gave me 'the talk', plus tried and tested coping mechanisms. On my part, I started to distance my Ghanaian home life from my English school life. From the teachers, there was often surprise at my intelligence, and I sometimes felt like I wasn't supported as much as some of my classmates. Luckily for me – perhaps unluckily – because I was able to pick things up very quickly, I didn't think this unconfirmed worse treatment had any effect on me. I got into the local grammar school and was very excited to find another black girl in my class. Again,

on the teaching front, I was often left to hide under the radar. With the exception of a few good teachers, most were happy to assume I wasn't worth any extra effort. And I *hated* homework (still do!) so there were lots of excited exclamations when this average B student pulled out As and A*s for GCSEs. They didn't connect back to the countless parents' evenings when they were told they needed to push me! A Levels we can discuss another day when I have a bigger word count! Despite how it sounds, reading it back now, my life trajectory always felt like an obvious straight line, with a science focus: GCSEs > A levels > degree > Imperial College London (research technician).

A few years into working at Imperial College, I was finally convinced to take on a PhD. I'd had offers before, but I really didn't fancy writing a thesis . . . #MegaHomework! From this acceptance I assumed my next steps would be obvious: PhD > Post=Doc > 'Academic' > Professor. But life had other plans. After a serious health condition, plus other factors, I found myself nearing the end of my contract, as I was nearing the end of 'the thesis write-up'. I had to decide if I was going to pursue a career in academia. We love our stats, so

WHAT I NEEDED WAS AN ENVIRONMENT WHERE I FELT I WOULD BE SUPPORTED AND

I did a quick search on how many black female professors we had. The answer was 'zero'. I changed my career path toward administration. Some things I should have noted: 'zero' included lecturers and readers.

A decade later, there are only thirty-five black female professors in the whole of the UK, and they make up 0 per cent of senior university leadership roles. What I needed was an environment where I felt I would be supported and encouraged to pursue and thrive, while striving to achieve to the top levels in my field. And that is my objective now for those coming through. With my different roles I have been challenging from all angles, with the goal to help researchers make the decision to stay in academia.

Dr Sarah Essilfie-Quaye.
Project Manager in Research Strategy, Imperial College, London

Sarah is part of the Research Strategy Team, in the Faculty of Medicine, at Imperial College, London. She is also the cochair for Imperial As One, and the first point of contact for queries pertaining to the Wellcome Trust Institutional Strategic Support Fund.

ENCOURAGED
TO PURSUE AND THRIVE

Afterword

It has been painful to read some of the stories in our book. I have cried sometimes. Knowing that some of these stories have been voiced for the first time, the question came to my mind: Why didn't we express this suffering before? Why did we need to witness the barbarism of George Floyd's death to unleash these utterings?

I've asked that question of myself. The answer is painful for me to hear. I refused to express them because I was running away from addressing all those wasted years of trying to fit in; of trying to diminish who I really am; to be accepted; of hiding my unique qualities to fit in (I even lost some of my hair from chemical burns to my scalp while trying to make my hair palatable to the European white beauty aesthetic in my industry); of minimizing my voice to avoid the harsh light of the solo spotlight; of following the crowd to avoid otherness.

I needed to bury this pain so I didn't feel the trauma consciously, but now I know for real that whatever you run away from, *it* just gets stronger and faster and *it* will catch you in the end. George Floyd's murder is my end. No more running. I am 'at the end' and I am turning and facing *it*. And hey, now the tears have dried it feels good. I feel strong and powerful and so much faster than *it*. To quote many retired athletes, 'I have hung up my spikes.'

I am not a writer, and at the start of 2020 I would never have imagined Suzette and I would put together this book. I don't know when I first started to believe in 'winter always turns to spring', but I do. The winter is the pain of 2020 outside and inside of me. 2021 will be the spring.

I applaud and celebrate every single person who contributed to *Still Breathing*. The effect of racism on their lives is traumatic.

This book is a declaration that no matter how much racism has tried to destroy us and produce causes for self-hatred, racism (*it*) will not succeed. We will not be defeated.

Suzanne

For me this anthology was born out of resistance to racism, out of a need to turn poison into medicine. It was created to share stories of resilience, to encourage the young to use their voice to stand against prejudice and injustice. To encourage them not to be defined by a would-be oppressor. That living your life, your joy, is your birthright.

For me, this anthology is a reminder that I must define myself or lose myself to the world.

Remember, black children, that you are beautiful.

In love & strength

Suzette

We want to thank everyone who trusted us with their intimate experiences. We apologize for the audacity of asking, as we realize how difficult and painful it has been to put them down on paper. We are eternally grateful for them allowing us to expand our hearts. We have learnt so much more: from our oldest contributor, Arthur Torrington, about our history, to one of our youngest, Elis James, about demonstrating independence and facing your enemies with courage. Sometimes, we felt like intruders reading them, but most of the time we felt like students. We have been given lessons in tenacity, pride, and resilience, against heartbreaking humiliation and, most of all, in surviving the injustices of racism.

So, thank you to all of the other ninety-eight voices. We are so proud and blessed to be part of such a wonderful and aspirational race of people. Thank you for entrusting us with your life experiences. They will remain in our hearts as a treasure that we will protect and hold dear.

Still Breathing heralds the spring.

Our Chosen Charity

We wanted this book to be of benefit, not just in the reading, but in the money it made. We knew we wanted a charity that would enrich the lives of those young children that we once were. We interviewed a number of charities and the one we chose firmly ticked that box.

Profits from the sales of this book will go to the Ashdon Jazz Academy.

The charity was started by Tricia Muirhead in 2015, following the tragic death of her daughter, Ashdon Muirhead, who ended her own life at the age of just 14 years. Ashdon struggled with peer pressure and aggression at school, and a lack of confidence about being herself in a society that pressurizes young women to be and act a certain way.

Tricia has made it her life's work to help girls fighting the same demons Ashdon struggled with. Since it was set up, the charity, working alongside a number of statutory and voluntary organizations, has helped hundreds of young girls through the provision of workshops, projects, drop-in sessions, retreats, and weekly Girls' Nights. The main work of the charity is to assign a mentor with a mentee on a 1:1 basis. They meet, or speak regularly, and empower confidence, develop personal skills, help deal with the challenges, and are a listening ear.

Ashdon Muirhead

Acknowledgements

Rose Sandy, for seeing our vision and making it a reality.

The team at HarperCollins, for holding our hand during the process.

Our friends and families, who we badgered to come up with suggestions for contributors.

Our team of youthful helpers, who lighten our paths every day: Elliot Leachman, for allowing us to pick his brain about graphics and artwork; Lois Uduje for her calming gaze over our admin; and Viva Rademacher for her research skills.

Index

Index

Photography Credits

Kwame Kwei-Armah
© Kwame Kwei-Armah

Damian Paul Daniel
© Damian Paul Daniel

Pamela Nompumelelo Nomvete
© Pamela Nompumelelo Nomvete

Jason Pennycooke © Jason Pennycooke

Sharon D. Clarke © Sharon D. Clarke

Halina Edwards © Avesta Keshtmand

Sheda of Holda Poetry
© Sheda of Holda Poetry

Trish Cooke © Trish Cooke

Jocelyn Esien © Jocelyn Esien

Sharon Walters © Sharon Walters

Josephine Melville © Josephine Melville

Rakie Ayola © Rakie Ayola

Errol Donald © Errol Donald

Veronica McKenzie © Veronica McKenzie

Suzanne Packer © Suzanne Packer

Mzz Kimberley © Mzz Kimberley

Judith Jacob ©Gemini Photography UK

Josette Bushell-Mingo
© Josette Bushell-Mingo

Michael Obiora © Michael Obiora

Benedicta Makeri © Benedicta Makeri

Stevie Basaula © Suzette Llewellyn

Beverley Knight © Beverley Knight

Suzette Llewellyn © Max A Hatter

Sistren © Sistren

Merissa Hylton © Ekaterina Mamontova

Neequaye 'Dreph' Dsane
© Neequaye 'Dreph' Dsane

Jacob V. Joyce © Jacob V. Joyce

Lettie Precious © Lettie Precious

Chinonyerem Odimba
© Chinonyerem Odimba

Treva Etienne © Treva Etienne

Elliot Leachman © Elliot Leachman

Bumi Thomas © Max A Hatter

Beverley Michaels © Beverley Michaels

Revd Dr Sharon Prentis
© Revd Dr Sharon Prentis

Ekow Suancheé © Ekow Suancheé

Dame Elizabeth Anionwu
© Dame Elizabeth Anionwu

Andrez Harriott © Andrez Harriott

Busayo Twins © Busayo Twins

Jacqueline Antoine © Jacqueline Antoine

Elis Jones © Elis Jones

Dr Lorna Cork © Dr Lorna Cork

Dr Robert Beckford © Dr Robert Beckford

Carmen Smart © Carmen Smart

Dr Vanessa Apea © Dr Vanessa Apea

Rev. Jide Macaulay © Rev. Jide Macaulay

Nigel Walker © Nigel Walker

Teleica Kirkland © Teleica Kirkland

Fiona Compton © Fiona Compton

Maureen Nassoro © Maureen Nassoro

Sonia Obasogie © Sonia Obasogie

Dr Owen Williams © Dr Owen Williams

Beverley Randall © Beverley Randall

Colton Belgrave © Colton Belgrave

Joyce Akpogheneta
© Joyce Akpogheneta

Angela Jackson © Angela Jackson

Kai Harper © Kai Harper

Yaw Amankona © Yaw Amankona

Pamela Franklin ©Aida Silvestri

Bishop Rose © Bishop Rose

Michelle Griffith Robinson
© Michelle Griffith Robinson

Dr Judith Agwada-Akeru
© Dr Judith Agwada-Akeru

Tony Hendrickson © Tony Hendrickson

Phyll Opoku-Gyimah
© Phyll Opoku-Gyimah

Arthur Torrington © Arthur Torrington

Sharrion J. Francis © Pam Wrigley

Lord Paul Boateng © Lord Paul Boateng

M. Jay © M. Jay

Dotun Adebayo © Dotun Adebayo

Dawn Butler © Dawn Butler

Ali Abdi © Ali Abdi

Photography Credits

Hermon and Heroda Berhane
© Hermon and Heroda Berhane

Ron Shillingford © Ron Shillingford

Trevor Phillips © Trevor Phillips

Shaun Bailey ©Shaun Bailey

Pat Younge © Pat Younge

Patrick Vernon © Patrick Vernon

Nadine White © Nadine White

Vaughan Gething © Vaughan Gething

David Lammy © David Lammy

Marcia Degia © Marcia Degia

Bonnie Greer © Lanre Olagoke

Pam Wrigley © Pam Wrigley

Dean Alexander © Dean Alexander

Dr Faith Uwadiae © Dr Faith Uwadiae

Chef Orlando © Chef Orlando

Shereener Browne © Shereener Browne

Allan Willmot © Allan Willmot

Kayisha Payne © Kayisha Payne

Ray Emmet Brown © Ray Emmet Brown

Diana Dahlia © Diana Dahlia

Albert Amankona © Pam Wrigley

Kaya Lockiby-Belgrave
© Kaya Lockiby-Belgrave

Brendon Winter © Brendon Winter

Jackee Holder © Jackee Holder

Andrea E. L. Attipoe
© Andrea E. L. Attipoe

Sonia Campbell © Sonia Campbell

Kevin Maxwell © Kevin Maxwell

Professor Uzo Iwobi
© Professor Uzo Iwobi

Bernadette Thompson
© Bernadette Thompson

Dr Sarah Essilfie-Quaye
© Dr Sarah Essilfie-Quaye

Ashdon Muirhead © Patricia Muirhead